About *JERRY FORD: UP CLOSE*

"A useful compilation of facts on Ford's life and political career . . . Americans will read it with considerable interest." *John Barkham Reviews*

"Written straightforwardly and packed with information . . . the book will bear re-reading." *Fort Worth Press*

About BUD VESTAL

Bud Vestal, veteran Grand Rapids reporter, has covered both national and international news for the prizewinning Booth newspaper chain and has known Gerald Ford since 1948.

D1381956

JERRY FORD
Up Close

BUD VESTAL

A BERKLEY MEDALLION BOOK
PUBLISHED BY COWARD, McCANN & GEOGHEGAN, INC.
DISTRIBUTED BY BERKLEY PUBLISHING CORPORATION

Coward, McCann & Geoghegan
200 Madison Avenue
New York, New York 10016

Library of Congress Catalog Card Number: 74-78008

SBN 425-02749-X

BERKLEY MEDALLION BOOKS are published by
Berkley Publishing Corporation
200 Madison Avenue
New York, N.Y. 10016

Coward, McCann & Geoghegan
200 Madison Avenue
New York, New York 10016

BERKLEY MEDALLION BOOKS ® TM 757,375

Printed in the United States of America

Coward, McCann & Geoghegan/Berkley Medallion Edition,
OCTOBER, 1974

Photographs courtesy of the Ford family.

CONTENTS

Prologue

It began on October 10, 1973. Vice President Spiro T. Agnew resigned from office and went to court to plead no contest to a charge of income-tax evasion, a felony under federal law, and pay a fine. He had faced more than forty charges of conspiracy, bribery and tax fraud, but he resorted to the old American custom of plea bargaining to avoid months if not years in the trial courts and an agony of scandal for the nation. Also, quite possibly, to avoid prison.

On October 10 this writer was driving through Oklahoma, returning from a vacation in California. Just east of Tulsa the car radio began to blurt bulletins about Agnew. With my wife, Phillis, I listened, dangerously fascinated while traveling a busy highway at seventy miles an hour.

As with most Americans, my first thought was, "Agnew is just a crook after all."

Second: "Now who?"

"Nixon will appoint Jerry Ford," Phillis said with conviction.

A self-professed political expert, I recited the litany of why-nots and concluded, "Jerry is a square's square; it would be just too much, even for Nixon."

"That's just why," she replied. "Nixon needs somebody everybody knows is honest."

President Nixon announced just two days after Agnew's resignation that he would nominate a new Vice President, under the recently enacted Twenty-fifth Amendment to the U.S. Constitution. That nominee was the Minority Leader of the House, Republican Gerald Ford of Michigan. There followed one of the most exhaustive investigations of a man's life in American history. Everybody got in on it—the Rules Committee of the Senate, the Judiciary Committee of the House, and the FBI. Everyone ever associated with Ford was questioned about him.

But across the nation and even around the world there arose one question: Who is Jerry Ford, what kind of man is he, what kind of President would he make? Even in Michigan no library had a book about Ford. Outside of Congress, Ford's fifth congressional district in Michigan, and Republican party officials, Ford really was unknown. And at any moment Ford could become President by any one of three ways—impeachment and conviction of Nixon, his resignation or his death.

Opinion polls showed Nixon's popularity plummeting disastrously. Nixon had compounded the shock set off by Agnew's resignation by firing Watergate special prosecutor Archibald Cox, just ten days after Agnew's exit. The "Saturday night massacre," as government bureaucrats and newsmen began to call Cox's firing, electrified Americans. There followed, in the words of new presidential staff chief Alexander Haig, "a firestorm" of public protest. In a matter of days more than 300,000 individual telegrams and letters were received at the White House or at the Capitol. Most strongly disapproved the "massacre."

Democrats, labor leaders, liberals of every description, cried out for impeachment. Even some Republican Congressmen, some Republican Governors and other party leaders expressed public disapproval. Privately, one Republican put it this way: "Nixon told us there wouldn't be any more bombs in the Watergate investigation, and then he set off one of the worst bombs of all without any warning or concern for his party, with an election year coming up."

1 The Unknown Man

In the United States' unique system of government Gerald Ford, until October of 1973, was one of the most powerful yet unknown leaders. He had represented two Michigan counties, where the biggest vote he ever got was 131,461. Now, in a few minutes, he would take the second highest office in a nation of more than 210 million.

For twenty-five years he had prepared himself for leadership; he had studied government night and day, always planning how to achieve the next rung up the ladder and what to do when he got there. But few knew it. The major news media applauded his honesty, candor and humility—at the same time listing the reasons he should be humble. A leading journal of foreign opinion deplored the spectacle of a great nation wracked by scandal turning to "a mediocrity" for solace. Ford was aware of all this.

He was sixty. He was also a very strong man in all senses of the word. He stood straight, over six feet tall and not much heavier than when he had played football thirty-nine years earlier. His face was bony, square-jawed, almost forbidding in repose. His wide smile showed big, even teeth, and it flashed like a light suddenly turned on. There was something about the nose, obviously damaged on the football field, something about the wide mouth and stern brow—like an old portrait of George Washington in the National Gallery of Art.

But he was no Washington, nor a Lincoln, he admitted. Not a Harry Truman by nine country miles, nor a Calvin Coolidge, although critics termed him conservative enough.

He was himself and he had spent sixty years shaping that self. The sophisticates who would try to limn his character were frustrated because he was so normal, so sane. History was going mad in 1973. Why didn't this man manifest some flaw, some fear or at least a little self-doubt? Why, the man was enjoying it! He was proud to be Vice President!

At 6:10 P.M., December 6, 1973, Gerald Rudolph Ford, Jr., raised his right hand in the U.S. House of Representatives, where he had spent twenty-five years working toward but never getting the top office of Speaker, and became Vice President of the United States.

His wife, Elizabeth, stood beside Chief Justice Warren E. Burger, who administered the oath. President Nixon stood behind Ford—actually and figuratively. "It's Jerry's day," Nixon commented. Ford spoke the oath loud and clear in his Midwestern accent. His voice always carried well: It was a little higher pitched than might be expected from such a sturdy chest and it had a tendency to sharp rather than flat. He fluffed his lines just once, in the phrase "I will well and faithfully discharge." Justice Burger repeated the phrase and Ford corrected himself.

Speaker Carl Albert presided. He had given the Ford family his special gallery seats, where the Fords' four children, Michael, John, Steven, and Susan, sat alongside Mrs. Nixon and the President's chief of staff, General Alexander M. Haig, Jr. Susan shed a few tears; her brothers paid close attention to the ceremony. Mrs. Nixon had a sweet-sad smile on her gaunt face: Her husband also had been a Vice President. An historian would have given much to know her thoughts in those moments.

There were 1,500 persons packed into the House chamber, including Representatives, Senators, ambassadors of foreign nations, and a delegation of more than 400 Michigan friends. All applauded loudly. "Fishbait" Miller, veteran sergeant at arms, said it was the biggest audience he could remember.

Immediately after the oath-taking ceremony Speaker Albert announced his "high personal honor of presenting to you a dear friend and former colleague, whom we shall all miss but whom we all congratulate, the Vice President of the United States." There was another diapason of applause.

Ford spoke approximately seven minutes. He thanked everyone present for being so kind to just plain Jerry Ford, then uttered an unexpectedly humorous but typically Fordian quip: "I'm a Ford, not a Lincoln. My addresses will never be as eloquent." (You can bet the White House speech writers had not created that line, although they would move in on Ford soon enough.)

Ford's first pledge was, "Mr. President, you have my support and my loyalty." This was no news to Nixon nor to the merest page at rear of the chamber. Loyalty was exactly why Ford was the new Vice President.

Only once did the inner Ford come through: His voice broke when he said in typical Ford syntax, "For standing by my side, as she always has, there are no words to tell you, my dear wife and mother of our four wonderful children, how much their being here means to me." No tears were on Elizabeth Ford's face, even then. One felt she had shed tears for sufficient cause, but at fifty-five was not about to weep at a political ceremony. There was something haunting

11

in her features, as with Mrs. Nixon's. American politics takes a toll on a wife.

Ford, led by Speaker Albert, was escorted to the U.S. Senate to be formally presented and to be reminded by Majority Leader Mike Mansfield, "Here, presiding officers are to be seen and not heard, unlike the House where the speaker's gavel is like a thunderclap."

Ford took this with a smile and commenced his brief greeting to the Senators with the words: "A funny thing happened to me on the way to becoming Speaker of the House."

Then after a rest in his House office, the new Vice President and his family went to what had been planned as "a Michigan party" in the Capitol Hill Club, a plush private clubhouse for Republican Congressmen. About 400 were expected. More than 1,000 tried to reach the receiving line, and many failed to get near the head of it, where Ford shook hands and thanked his friends for coming. Speaker Albert stood beside him like a happy little beaver. Albert had been next in line of succession to the presidency since October 10—a fact that Democratic party strategists didn't like to live with. And next in line after Albert had been Senator James O. Eastland of Mississippi, the cotton baron, a thought that gave such Northern liberals as Senator Philip A. Hart of Michigan the midnight shakes. (There were so many reasons to rejoice over Jerry as VP!)

Hart came to the party, of course. He had surprised his fellow liberals in Washington by declaring publicly he would welcome Nixon's resignation because he would "feel safer at night" with Ford in the White House. Hart stood to one side from the notables in the receiving line, watching, a wan smile on his bearded face. Michigan Democrats wished he would get rid of the beard because beards had become the symbol of ultraliberalism in their circles, and they were trying hard to forget George McGovern. Hart didn't care: He had confided to close friends he did not intend to seek reelection in 1976.

Hart was by no means the only Democrat who came to honor Jerry at twenty dollars a ticket. Also arriving was Michigan's other Congressman Ford—William D. Ford, of Michigan's fifteenth district in the Detroit suburbs. This Ford joked that he wanted "to see how Republicans live." Democrat James G. O'Hara also came by to salute Jerry. The busing issue had made common cause between the liberal anti-busing O'Hara and the conservative Ford.

There were few blacks, very few. Missing were Michigan's two blacks in Congress, veteran Charles Diggs, Jr., and John Conyers, Jr., of Detroit. Both moved in a different world from that of Jerry Ford.

The party was a happy one, reminiscent of television's *This Is Your Life* program. There were Mr. and Mrs. John B. Martin, Jr., and Mr. and Mrs. Paul G. Goebel, who with Jerry were charter members of the old Grand Rapids-Kent County Home Front political organization. Also attending was John Milanowski, who had been Jerry's first administrative aide in Congress and who was now federal district attorney for West Michigan, thanks to Jerry Ford. And there was former Michigan Governor George Romney—the Mormon on horseback who became a presidential front-runner in 1967 and then went downhill all the way to the 1968 New Hampshire presidential primary campaign.

There were reminiscences, as Jerry's friends reconvened. Goebel recalled the first time he had ever met Ford. He had attended the University of Michigan ten years before Jerry and was an all-conference end

13

in football. He liked to officiate at football games and once did so at a game in which Jerry's champion South High School had played. Goebel said Jerry had a problem with an opponent and both players were getting testy. He warned them, but in a pileup the tormenting opponent did something Jerry didn't like. Jerry came up to his feet, gave what Goebel said was "a good, hard belt in the chops" and knocked the other player down. "You're out of this game," Goebel shouted and Jerry walked off the field "without argument."

Ford himself wore a broad grin throughout the party, enjoying it despite fatigue. When asked his thoughts during the swearing-in ceremony, he said, "I was trying to remember my lines; I guess I blew them once, though." And he laughed heartily. It was no time to talk of serious matters. That would come later. Jerry Ford was going to be a very busy man trying to do for a President some things the President was peculiarly unable to do for himself.

Across the country this particular night there was, metaphorically, a national sigh of relief. The nation, with its unique form of federal government, had a new Vice President. A most presentable one, investigated right down to his bills at the tailor by Federal Bureau of Investigation agents and certified clean. This was a Vice President who actually liked Congress and got along well with its members, who even liked news reporters and was candid about himself. Never mind how he would do as President—that question could come later. A vacuum had been filled, a shock abated.

2 Why Ford?

Why this man over any other? Why nominate Jerry Ford, the big jock, the athlete who didn't look his sixty years, the politician who could have been a preacher and thought the same set of morals would work for both? Why this legislative technician who was known to think for himself on occasion, sometimes with (politically) disastrous results?

The answers are simple and several; they explain why my wife could predict Ford's nomination while the Manchester *Guardian* could not. One must understand the simplicities of a political system as well as the intricacies.

Trust: If Ford gave his word, he kept it.

Liking: Ford and Nixon had met after Nixon's first term in the House of Representatives. They had come to know and like each other. They were lawyers, conservative at heart when still young men; they saw things with the same eyes.

Obedience: Ford might disagree but he wouldn't insist on going to the Supreme Court with his own judgment.

And on the other hand, who were the alternatives? The stalwart former Defense Secretary Mel Laird, as Jerry Ford knew, had been among the few men considered. But Laird in recent times had disagreed with Nixon's judgments, had said so, and had pressed his point. Laird wanted out; Ford was ambitious for a bigger role.

Senator Robert P. Griffin of Michigan? He had led opposition to Nixon Supreme Court nominee Haynsworth. Furthermore, Griffin had opposed some Nixon program legislation: His loyalty as measured in voting record was 77 percent; Ford's was better than 90.

How about Ronald Reagan, Governor of Nixon's home state of California? Completely unrealistic: It could result in handing "Dutch" the 1976 presidential nomination on a platter, much too important a gem to be given away prematurely.

Governor Nelson Rockefeller of New York, soon to resign his office and launch his own "exploratory" presidential campaign? The same prime reason applied, plus some other good ones. Enough to say Nixon didn't like Rockefeller, the rich liberal who had spoken against the will of the 1964 Republican national convention—refusing to let it hoot him off the podium because he didn't like Barry Goldwater. Rockefeller was turning conservative too late.

John B. Connally, the super-slick Texas oil lawyer who converted to Republicanism just after the roof fell in on the Nixon administration? As the saying has it, the Catholic church accepts converts, too, but it doesn't make them cardinals the next day.

Senator Jacob K. Javits of New York? One of the most distinguished Jews in American government. But wait a moment: Can one imagine Nixon appointing an intellectual, a liberal, to be one heartbeat away from the presidency? The voter from Anaheim, Peoria or Okemos could not; Mrs. Nixon herself probably could not. Besides, Mrs. Javits was an Eastern socialite beauty. One should always look to the wife as well as the man and ask, Will she sell in Peoria?

Jerry Ford had all the pluses and very few minuses. He had never authored a major program of legislation on his own, never made an enemy needlessly, never joined the wrong cause or crusade, had never been tainted by liberal political commitments, seldom disagreed with Nixon programs.

The President moved quickly following Agnew's fall. Ford said in retrospect he should have known by 11:00 A.M., October 12, that he was chosen, because of the nature of the telephone calls from the White House. Ford said it really dawned on him that he was chosen when he entered the White House that evening and Nixon told Ollie Atkins, chief White House photographer, "make this a good picture of Jerry and me—it could be important some day."

The President had decreed a ceremony: The presence of the vice-presidential eligibles, military aides, live television coverage, a band, refreshment at the ready but not where cameras would photograph it. Hoked up, corny, almost mock-heroic, it was like a family reunion in formal dress. But in fairness, a Vice President had never been picked this way before so there was no protocol, no precedent. Nixon had full license to improvise and he did, for the benefit of many millions watching their TV sets.

Smiles, applause and moisture at the corners of the eyes followed when Nixon turned to Ford and uttered his name. Ford's brief acknowledgment certainly was unrehearsed. It was a declaration of fealty that sounded like a mixture of the Boy Scout pledge and the oath to uphold the Constitution. But it was as sincere as Ford's obvious happiness and pride in having been chosen.

For a few weeks Ford had the best of two worlds. He was still House Minority Leader and would be until exhaustive investigation by the FBI, until the House Judiciary and Senate Rules committees had held their hearings, received the FBI reports, questioned him about everything the members could possibly think of. And then a simple majority vote of both House and Senate would make him Vice President under the Twenty-fifth Amendment.

Ford himself had no worries on any point because he knew he had a clean record; most Congressmen were sure of it, too, and that was all the more reason for an exhaustive investigation. It wasn't enough that Congress be sure: The American people and the world had to be assured the man was truly "Mister Clean."

At one time more than 430 FBI agents across the nation worked on the investigation. It covered everything imaginable and many things improbable. An agent went to the tailor in Grand Rapids who for twenty-five years had made most of the clothing Ford wore. The tailor, an imaginative man named Lloyd Lievense, had kept a record of every coat, suit and pair of trousers. He had also urged Ford to wear brighter, more informal clothing long before the so-called mod fashions had become popular. No luck: Ford was not "mod" in taste.

"I wouldn't call his taste farmerish . . . but on the other hand . . ." Lievense fell silent when asked to characterize Ford's severe clothing styles. "Well, I notice since his nomination that he's loosening up a little," Lievense added. "You can see that on color television." Ford, it seems, had commenced buying clothing in Washington after his nomination.

And what did the FBI agent want to know from the tailor? "How did he pay for the clothes?"

"He didn't," Lievense said with a slightly theatrical pause. "His wife did. He never got a new suit from me that she didn't make him come and get on his visits to Grand Rapids. They were always think-

18

ing of each other first; he bought her dresses in Washington stores, when he saw one he liked."

The FBI's raw file, its stack of reports from such exhaustive research, must have taken a yardstick to measure. And it was just one part of the vetting of Ford for the vice presidency, the ascertaining from the policeman's point of view that Ford had never been guilty of violent crime, moral turpitude, larceny by conversion, grand theft or fraud, mopery or stealing from the church poor box.

Much broader inquiry came during hearings by the House Judiciary and Senate Rules committees. The members and other Congressmen had questions about Ford's political history and current beliefs; so did leaders of the Americans for Democratic Action, National Association for the Advancement of Colored People and others.

Clarence Mitchell, director of the NAACP's Washington bureau, testified he felt Ford had a "narrow-gage" approach to civil rights legislation. Dr. Lyman Parks, Grand Rapids' first black mayor, stated in a letter read into the record by Senator Griffin that Ford's help in getting federal aid made possible a model-cities program of benefit to disadvantaged people. A letter from Leonard Woodcock, president of the United Auto Workers union, supported Ford for the nomination. Testimony by Congressman John Conyers, a black representing a Detroit district, recited some of Ford's voting record on social and civil rights legislation; Conyers termed Ford "insensitive to the needs of the people."

There was testimony concerning Ford's attack in 1970 on Supreme Court Justice William O. Douglas; his support of the President's unsuccessful nomination of G. Harrold Carswell and Clement F. Haynsworth to the Supreme Court; his raising of funds (and they were considerable) for Republican congressional candidates—not only for himself but for the Republican Congressional Boosters Club. There was testimony that he had recommended a Boosters contributor for an ambassadorship; that he had received contributions from the milk industry and in 1971 a $1,500 honorarium from the Associated Milk Producers to speak at their national convention. Ford noted that the paid convention speakers list included "ten or twenty Congressmen—an equal number of Republicans and Democrats."

The inquiry turned to other matters. It was established that Ford had used the multiple-committee system in fund-raising, as had many other candidates. That in his twenty-five years in the House he had had a good attendance and voting record, and more often voted with conservatives. That he had had an unfortunate association with a lobbyist named Robert N. Winter-Berger, who had made many allegations about Ford in a book on Washington graft. Winter-Berger testified at length. Later his testimony was submitted to the Justice Department to determine if he had committed perjury. That episode is a story in itself, to be told later in this book.

So it went, from October 12 until the end of November. The FBI report—not the whole raw file but the report—was 1,400 pages long. The tons of paper used in the investigation of Ford offered a treasure trove for future doctoral candidates in political history.

Most of those involved in the investigation, Ford included, grew weary of the detail, the recitation of names, dates, amounts, the praise and the criticism, the picking apart of a man's public career almost dollar by dollar, day by day. It was established, too, that at the age of sixty Ford was worth perhaps $250,000, counting two homes.

But they wanted to do it right. It was the first time in American political history Congress had to approve or reject a presidential nomination for Vice President under the Twenty-fifth Amendment, the "Kennedy amendment," adopted after the assassination in Dallas. Conservative he might be, but Ford held up under scrutiny.

There were stories like this—once, at a University of Michigan homecoming, a former 1934 football teammate had celebrated too much the night before. The morning of the game Ford got him up, gave him the black-coffee-and-shower treatment, and got him dressed and to the stadium with the help of a companion, one on each side for support. Entering the stadium, they encountered University of Michigan President Harlan Hatcher. Jerry Ford greeted him respectfully and then carefully introduced "my good friend." His buddy still didn't know what was going on. Later, when asked why such concern and effort in "getting a drunk to a game," Ford replied simply, "He is one of my best friends." Years afterward Ford, a little ruefully, corroborated the story. "You don't go back on a friend," he insisted again.

Nixon knew this aspect of Ford's character from old association when both had been in the House. And he could well calculate how much loyalty Ford would give to a friend who happened to be President of the United States. The President didn't consider many men for the job—Ford thought "about five"— nor did he take long deciding.

3 Idyll and Agony

White House strategists planned the Dick and Jerry Show to be the hottest production since Nixon's "Checkers" speech: a duo performance, with Jerry doing much of the talking and his President looking on, beaming, as if to say, "That's my boy."

The critics of the time were a confused group. And no wonder. The Watergate investigations and prosecutions were bearing new fruit daily. The most respected political observers saw the scandal closing around the President, and many predicted he had only months left in office. Nixon changed his strategy and aborted "Operation Candor" so suddenly Ford was still talking about "compromise" on White House tapes and documents while White House press secretary Ronald Ziegler was saying contrition was out.

It was a strange series of events, some important and some trivial; it was difficult to discern which was which. Small wonder it produced a strange phenomenon in journalism: The many articles and broadcasts about Ford ran a gamut from harshness to praise to sharp criticism to wait-a-minute-let's-analyze-this.

Ford didn't complain about his press reviews—a lifetime habit never to complain or look back—he just kept on holding press conferences and giving interviews. He never in his life tried to outsmart anybody. But if from intellectual hubris a tormentor gave him a chance, Jerry would outdumb him, swiftly and deadpan. It might be days before the attacker would realize he'd been had. Professional pols appreciate the difference between "outsmart" and "outdumb," and the more professional they are, the more they prefer the latter. (In his last press conference of 1973 Nixon had tried to outsmart Clark Mollenhoff, veteran Capitol correspondent and Pulitzer-prize winner; he had sounded like a fishwife.)

Only one analyst troubled to point out this aspect of Ford's character during his first seventy days as Vice President. While others called the man simple, Charlie McCollum in *New Times* magazine gave a caveat. He said Ford was a limited man with no great intellect or dream for America. But Ford knew it, said McCollum, and furthermore was "shrewd, politically sharp" and had a "precise grasp of where his limitations lie and just exactly where he wants to go." He said there was ambition in Ford's soul, of the kind that moved Ford ahead "one small step at a time, never straining his resources or his totally ingratiating manner."

Yes, Vice President Ford was among other things a gentleman. A fact that many forgot to mention. Not the courtly, sweeping-gesture gentleman the South could train, just quietly considerate of other humans' need for self-respect. He really liked people, but it wasn't in him to be effusive about it.

Press Secretary Paul Miltich warned anyone who would listen that although Ford was not an orator or even a raconteur, he was almost always the center of attention after entering a room, and in a "one-on-one situation would charm you out of your socks."

Regardless of who was right, it was a wonder Ford could keep calm the first few weeks after he took the oath of office December 6. Just moving his office from the House wing of the Capitol to the Old Executive

Office Building was a wrench. But they dismantled Ford's perfect people-pleasing machine of eighteen people and in eight weeks built a new one numbering fifty-four staff members, many of whom had assignments that were, in essence, to protect Jerry Ford from something. To screen out acquaintances rather than usher them in; to save time that was now more precious than ever; to provide instant liaison with the White House. Some longtime associates and friends wanted to protect him from the White House; some, to protect him from the public; and others, to protect him from himself.

Congress was still in session and there was an omnibus energy-conservation bill to try to get through it. Congress kept at work right up to Christmas, but despite the efforts of Ford and most Republican Congressmen, the majority Democrats would not confer shotgun power over daylight saving, highway speed limits, gas rationing, fuel allocation. The feeling was the President could decree almost any one power singly by executive order or declaration of emergency, anyway. The mood of Congress was wait and see. And who knew when Watergate would blow the entire picture apart? One senator said the future was impossible to predict because "We're dealing with a centipede and who knows when the fiftieth shoe will drop?"

Ford had made definite plans for the annual family vacation at his chalet in Vail and was not about to change his plans. One well-wisher suggested in print that he stay in Washington and be federal regent while the President skipped off to his Key Biscayne or San Clemente home. As if Nixon would tolerate that or Ford were stupid enough to try to upstage the boss!

The Secret Service strongly urged Ford to fly in a

government aircraft, fuel shortage or no, to present a minimum security risk. He accepted. Just before Christmas the family bundled into the vice-presidential Jetstar at Andrews Air Force Base—with a dozen servicemen on holiday leave who needed rides from Washington to Denver or points west—and flew to Vail.

Shortly after their departure President Nixon and his family, plus an entourage of grim, unhappy Secret Service agents, unexpectedly boarded a United Airlines Jumbo jet to Los Angeles and San Clemente. The covert boarding at Dulles International Airport delayed the flight more than an hour, but the civilian passengers were almost unanimous in their delight when, near Los Angeles, the President left the first-class cabin to walk among them, shake hands and chat a moment. That was upstaging the whole country, with unexpected verve. (The President had earlier tossed out a red herring by ordering his staff to check how much fuel a chartered train would burn going to Miami.)

At San Clemente the President retreated and was seen no more until early January, when he returned to Washington in his Air Force One jet.

At Vail Ford sacrificed his family's cherished privacy at its only reunion of the year to mollify the small platoon of newsmen covering him. He submitted to press conferences, although he had little to say about government or public affairs at the moment. Press Secretary Miltich had stayed in Washington, and Ford made it politely clear without spelling it out that there would be no profound discourses, there would be a vacation.

When a public-opinion-poll report came out showing Ford ahead of any other Republican (including Nixon) as presidential preference, Ford's comment was typical: "When I read that, Betty pulled the covers over her head and said she was going to burn all the papers."

(Yes, after twenty-four years of marriage they slept together. Betty said her husband was "a good sleeper" but the events of December were observable: "One night I woke up and Jerry was talking in his sleep—he kept saying, 'Thank you, thank you, thank you.' He was in a receiving line.")

Christmas day the cameramen were allowed to photograph the present-opening around the Ford Christmas tree. Jerry got a robe, red-white-and-blue suspenders, supplies for his pipe-smoking habit of many years. During the vacation he also went off his diet a bit, ate some steaks and his favorite tossed salads with spicy dressing. (On returning to Washington he ruled that lunch for him henceforth would be his old standby to hold weight below 193 pounds—cottage cheese with ketchup.)

Having recorded Christmas, the newsmen interviewed the Fords' three sons and their daughter. The results were refreshing, more interesting than interviewing the Vice President. The young Fords were highly intelligent, thoughtful and responsive.

Michael, twenty-three, is the introspective Ford. A divinity student at a theological seminary near Boston, he is working for a master's degree in theology but has not yet decided his future. Although he wants no part of politics, he said his father was an inspiration to him. "He's a go-getter. When he skis, he skis hard. When he's with the family, he's with the family, hard. He goes at everything one hundred percent. It's helped me at times when I've been down— to pick myself up and go."

John, twenty-one, is a forestry student at Utah State. He had fought forest fires the previous summer and is studying watershed management. But he is also considering law school and is the only young Ford who does not rule out a political future. He just doesn't know, but he is thinking.

Steve, seventeen, couldn't wait for high school graduation in June, to go on to college and dental school. "A dentist can be his own man, set his own hours. I could never shuffle papers eight hours a day." He termed the Ford family life "a simple way of life" and feared that would have to change "if we moved to the White House."

Susan, sixteen, takes lessons in ballet and modern dance, likes skiing, cooking, stitchery, clothing. She has no career plan yet. She receives fan mail. She had worked in the White House book shop the previous summer. She is totally unspoiled. It is her privilege to baby Shan, the family's Siamese cat. She says she can talk easily with any of her three brothers. "We confide and let each other know when somebody has done wrong."

With such children as these Jerry and Betty Ford would never want jewels. But there was so little time and they all wanted to ski—except Mother—and laugh together and store memories for the coming twelvemonth. The next year would be different from any before, and it would not be an easy one. Even Susan's features showed a concern that was mature beyond her years.

And so the vacation ended. The family returned to Washington. Nobody talked about the Harris poll, which had just reported, among other things, that the American electorate wished, 45 percent to 31, that President Nixon would resign and let Ford take over.

On January 15 there was an assignment for the Vice President: Address the American Farm Bureau Federation's annual convention in Atlantic City. His speech began innocuously enough and then flopped with a louder report than the high-diving horse. He called the American farmer the unsung hero of the nation's economy, claimed that "on that score my legislative record speaks for itself." (Yes, some of his votes on farm legislation, farm lobbyists believed, had helped contribute to the "unsung hero" role. But never mind now, Ford was here as surrogate for the President.)

There was a problem, not material but mental: confidence in the presidency. According to some polls, it had seldom been lower. That's bad. But there's worse:

"A few extreme partisans seem determined to make it worse—some seem bent on stretching out the ordeal of Watergate for their own purposes, whatever they might be.

"While the Farm Bureau is meeting here to discuss solving some of the nation's problems, a coalition of groups like the AFL-CIO, Americans for Democratic Action and other powerful pressure organizations is waging a massive propaganda campaign against the President of the United States.

"And make no mistake about it—it is an all-out attack. Their aim is total victory . . . total defeat not only of President Nixon, but of the policies for which he stands.

"If they can crush the President and his philosophy, they are convinced they can then dominate the Congress, and through it, the nation.

"Should that day ever come—with the super-welfare-staters in control of Congress, and the White House neutralized as a balancing force—we can expect an avalanche of fresh government intervention in our economy, massive new government spending, higher taxes and a more rampant inflation.

"The majority of responsible, thinking Americans must not let it happen, and I don't believe they will. . . .

"The American people are telling their elected representatives again and again . . . settle Watergate. Write the last chapter; close the book and get on with the vital business of the nation. It is high time we did just that . . . time we got out of the rut of despair and self-doubt and back onto the high road of progress. . . .

"When you look back on the past years of the Nixon administration and think of the . . . honorable end to America's longest war . . . new and promising relationships with the People's Republic of China and the Soviet Union . . . groundwork for a lasting peace in the Middle East . . . and think of these really magnificent achievements, then Watergate no longer dominates the landscape. . . . Compared with these mountainous achievements, it's a tragic but grotesque sideshow."

He did not touch on the indictments. As a result of Watergate twenty-six people, including two members of the President's cabinet and his close adviser, John D. Ehrlichman, had been indicted; more indictments were expected. In a few weeks former presidential counsel John Dean would be disbarred pending sentence, and a popular White House aide, Egil "Bud" Krogh, would be sentenced to six months in jail for having directed the White House "plumbers." The plumbers had burglarized the Los Angeles office of Daniel Ellsberg's psychiatrist in an effort to find evidence to discredit the man who had leaked the Pentagon Papers.

Ford just stuck to his script.

The next day Ford received a telephone call in his office while I was conducting an interview with him.

29

He asked if I would mind stepping out of his office a moment. Press Secretary Miltich stepped out, too, and chatted in the outer office.

Ford's loud "thank you" came through the wall. We returned.

"That was the President," Ford said, smiling. "He liked my speech in Atlantic City."

"He should," I said.

"Yeah!" said Ford, with the faintest of knowing tones in his voice. Faint, but there.

Mrs. Ford commented later that she and Susan knew when they heard the speech broadcast that it must have come from the White House—it was phrased in language unfamiliar to anyone who had listened to Ford's speeches for years. But she agreed Jerry had never had much love for the ADA and probably meant just what he said.

Ford and his staff readily acknowledged that the speech had been written by White House speech writers. Ford was looking for two but had yet to hire any. Miltich was "too busy" to write speeches any longer, they all said.

The White House had anticipated he would be. On December 5 Miltich had been summoned to the White House to lunch with a battery of speech writers, who told him now busy he would be. They offered to do Ford's speeches as long as necessary. Miltich was harried dealing with a news-hungry press corps. He didn't write any more speeches. He could have done better by a mile with the Atlantic City speech. Railing at the ADA—an aging and sometimes overrated liberal's lobby—is one thing. Lumping George Meany's AFL-CIO with it, putting him in the same basket with people who had supported the presidential campaign of George McGovern, was unnecessary. Also dumb. Meany had forbidden the AFL-CIO to support McGovern and so had contributed to Nixon's 1972 landslide-mandate. Meany might be calling for Nixon's resignation or impeachment, but he was far from sympathetic with "pinkos and left-wing nuts," in union jargon.

No less significant an observer than William S. White called the speech nationally divisive. He called it a "grievous error" and urged Ford to "disentangle himself."

Ford stuck to his guns and said he would have said the same thing, although maybe in different words.

After the first White House denial of any plan to "compromise" on giving over tape recordings of presidential conversations with staff in the Oval Office or the more than 500 White House documents sought by Watergate investigators, Ford still mentioned hope of "compromise." He continued to be interviewed on set-piece televised programs, and some of the questions were set piece.

He sought to explain that it was just that he had urged and continued to urge on the President candor and speed in answering Watergate investigators' questions.

But "Operation Candor" had been terminated by the White House, the questioner would remind him, sometime during the Christmas vacation at San Clemente. Deputy White House Press Secretary Gerald L. Warren had made it official the same day as That Speech in Atlantic City: Nixon "believed he had answered all the questions."

How did one respond to that? If one were Vice President Ford, one didn't, and would not seek to extend the line of reasoning, or extrapolate any further.

31

He insisted there might be times he would disagree with his President; he intended to do so when he must.

What did they want? That Ford go to Atlantic City and tell the farmers the President was a bum and should be thrown out?

The furor lasted a week, a good lifespan for a purely political furor in early 1974. If Nixon had picked Ford as a lightning rod, he had picked a durable one.

The independent truckers' strike turned public attention to more tangible problems—getting food and fuel to remote villages, deciding whether to roll back diesel-fuel prices or permit freight-rate surcharges. States began calling out National Guard units to halt sabotage and shootings. The big meeting of petroleum-purchasing nations in Washington was coming near. Busy times.

Ford went to Chicago to speak at a football dinner, an event that brings out the nostalgia of old football players. "I'd like to take the whole United States into the locker room between halves," said Ford, to express how badly he wanted the people to start talking about "what's right with America."

Then came the special election in Ford's own fifth district of Michigan to fill his vacant seat in Congress. Republican Robert VanderLaan, State Senate Majority Leader, was expected to win handily, if not with the usual 60 percent or more of the vote Jerry Ford had always received. VanderLaan, a former teacher, had disassociated himself from Nixon, had the benefit of Ford's appearance on his behalf, plus a campaign visit by Elliot Richardson himself—the Nixon defier.

VanderLaan's opponent, Democrat Richard F.

VanderVeen, a lawyer, said the issue was confidence in the President. He said the election constituted a referendum on Nixon and Watergate. Furthermore, he cleverly called on the President to resign and "put Jerry in the White House."

VanderLaan, in fifteen elections, had never lost one. VanderVeen had never won election to any significant office; in 1958 he had run against Ford for Congress and Ford had won 63 percent of the vote. VanderVeen was fifty-one, a mild, polite and undramatic campaigner, the opposite of a fire-eater. A Caspar Milquetoast. VanderLaan was forty-two, vigorous, ambitious. He, too, was critical of Watergate and had urged full disclosure of information by the President. VanderVeen won with 55,008 votes to 46,158 for VanderLaan.

The voting history of the district alone is enough to explain Republicans' shock, locally and nationally. The first time Ford ran for Congress he received 62 percent of the total vote of the two major parties; in 1950 it jumped to 66 percent; the same in 1952; in 1954 it was 63 percent; in 1956, 67 percent; in 1960, 67 percent; the same in 1962; in 1964 (Johnson landslide year) it dropped to 61 percent; then in 1966 (Republican landslide) it reached an all-time high of more than 68 percent. Then it dropped again, but never below 60 percent. In 1972 it was a fraction more than 60 percent. The Democratic opponents had never been strong candidates but were always respected community leaders; they were not just pols or hacks, they were substantial people, well-liked in the community.

Now a chronic loser—VanderVeen had run for mayor as well as other offices—had taken a strong Republican candidate to the cleaners on one issue:

Watergate. VanderLaan lost in Grand Rapids, in both Kent and Ionia counties; he carried his hometown, Kentwood, by only 758 votes.

Watergate was a trigger-word. It meant high food prices to some; unemployment to others; "the mess in Washington" to many. VanderVeen had invited the voters to "send 'em a message in Washington." And the voters did.

Despite their gnawing fears and the warnings from Washington, Republicans really had not expected such a debacle. For sixty-four years a Republican had held the congressional seat and now it was going to a Democrat, who quite obviously would be a vote for impeachment of the President. It was little comfort that VanderVeen would have to run again in November to hold the seat.

The comment of Republican Governor William G. Milliken of Michigan, immediate past chairman of the Council of Republican Governors, was blunt: "I don't know how many people switched votes because of Watergate. I don't know how many sat home because of Watergate. And I don't know at this point how heavily local factors influenced the vote. But the fact is Dick VanderVeen, who was elected to a body that is to make a crucial decision in the aftermath of Watergate, campaigned to make the election a referendum on Watergate.

"The fact is, the plague of Watergate has struck the heartland of America," Milliken concluded glumly. He, like Ford, had long urged on Nixon a course of candor and "full disclosure," as recently as the Republican Governors' conference, at which Nixon had promised "no more bombs."

The Grand Rapids *Press,* which had supported VanderLaan, said editorially: "The voters are deeply disillusioned with the Nixon administration. The

Republican party is in trouble—not just here but nationally. It is apparent that voters have had their fill of an administration which preaches law and order but whose highest officials condone breaking and entering and other unlawful acts; an administration which sympathizes with the tax burdens of the middle class, but whose President pays only token taxes on a government salary of $250,000; an administration which pays lip service to balanced budgets, but whose grossest national products are inflation and unemployment; an administration whose President views his purposes so important that he can operate above the law.

"As for our endorsement last week of Republican Robert VanderLaan, the *Press* is eating crow . . . and it ain't that bad!"

Vice President Ford himself had an immediate, sad reaction. He said he was shocked. Later he said he would inform the President that while Watergate was a factor, inflation and unemployment, fears of recession, were more important in deciding the outcome of the fifth-district election.

Other elections were to come all around the nation and also in Michigan's eighth district on the eastern side of the state, a marginal district with many more voters who normally voted Democratic. Democrats looked to pick up as many as forty new seats in the House of Representatives by the time the November election returns were counted.

A fiction writer could not have picked a symbol that would hurt Republicans more than the fifth-district election. Political writers from throughout the nation converged on Grand Rapids to find out what had happened. Suddenly the Grand Rapids area was much more than just the hometown of Jerry Ford. It was a bench mark in modern Republican history that called for a new survey. Something out there (in the boondocks, as they thought of it) was going on.

The Dick and Jerry show was still running. They were toughing it out on the Potomac, and damn the first man to cry quit. Most critics felt it couldn't possibly last the better part of three years, especially those who did not see logic in politics but saw it as tragedy, comedy or satire. Sooner or later there would have to be a resolution of the action, a catharsis, an end to a very strange agony.

4   The Staff

As a rookie Congressman Ford had opened shop
with a staff of three. On becoming Vice President he
had available to him approximately a million dollars
a year office-salary allowance and a table of organization authorizing approximately sixty warm bodies.
Enough, a taxpayer might think, to keep a king's
court functioning.

But, among others, one lesson of the Watergate
scandal was that a big staff of bright minds can get
the boss into so much trouble he must spend half his
time just trying to reorganize and survive. There is
an old saying in elective politics about the fate of a
Biblical character who "leaned on his staff and died."

Ford had built a staff of eighteen people he knew
and trusted. It was heavy on Michigan rather than
Washington origins, in keeping with Ford's style. He
took this staff with him as a nucleus when he moved
from cramped quarters in the Capitol to the Old Executive Office Building. Ford was given a large suite
of offices (with kitchen, even) on the second floor exactly above President Nixon's first-floor sanctum.
The White House took a direct hand in fleshing out
his staff, beginning with a squad of ultrapolite, hy-
perefficient military aides.

There were new titles for some: Robert Hartmann, his administrative aide, became "chief of
staff." Press Secretary Paul Miltich kept the same
title but quickly got an assistant, John W. "Bill"

Roberts, with a broadcast-news-media background (*Time-Life* network). The whole process was done in haste. The day after he was nominated Ford called Grand Rapids to ask a former political-science student-intern, as colleges called them, to come back on the staff full-time rather than pursue work for a graduate degree in political science. Miss Gail Raiman, twenty-three, daughter of Grand Rapids surgeon Robert J. Raiman, caught the next plane for Washington to be a receptionist-secretary in Hartmann's office. All indications were she would know more in a twelvemonth about practical politics than a professor at her alma mater, the prestigious Kalamazoo College.

Whether the number was eighteen or sixty, each staff member would have his or her own perception of Jerry Ford, and a distinct relationship with him. Ford's relationships with his own people remained "one on one" in the political vernacular, just as with his constituents and his friends in Congress.

A former Washington correspondent for the Los Angeles *Times* who had turned political professional and moved from one job to a better one as the opportunity came, Hartmann, at fifty-six, had been in Washington many years. His own politics were conservative Republican. He had known Nixon in the old California days; he had covered state politics when Nixon was starting his climb. Hartmann was as canny as a riverboat gambler; he could talk political strategy with Republican staffers in the White House, be a basilisk to newsmen who wrote critically; devise strategy for attacking the Johnson administration, for building a better Republican party image. Political hackery, yes, but as staff chief to the Vice President, his salary surpassed $40,000 a year.

Hartmann had first met Ford at Washington

parties. At the time he was hired by the House Republican Conference to assist Mel Laird and Ford, in 1966, he had known Laird longer and better. When Laird became Secretary of Defense, Hartmann went on Ford's staff full-time, still marveling at what he saw in the man.

"Calvinistic," Hartmann once commented in describing Ford's stern code of personal conduct. He said that Ford, because of his loyalty, took much longer than others to become disillusioned with Agnew but "left Agnew completely" when in one bitter moment he learned "Agnew had looked him in the eye and lied to him."

Therefore, Hartmann believed there was a simple answer to the question of how long Ford would remain loyal to Nixon. Until and unless Ford came to believe the President had not told, was not telling, the truth to Ford. Then the loss of loyalty would be total. A good judgment and another way of saying that Ford's Calvinistic ethics demand of a subordinate total loyalty to the leader—or none at all. Partial loyalty would be impossible.

The tapes? Hartmann laughed. "I think I'd like to have tapes myself. I want to know what's going on in the office."

Taking all income-tax deductions possible? "We all do that," Hartmann said. "The weight of those things is not enough to shake his loyalty."

But Hartmann the professional pol felt that Ford might remain loyal too long for his own good because in his, Hartmann's, judgment, the total situation in the White House was "unraveling like a double-knit jacket once a tear starts: It may have gone too far to be reversed. I wonder if it won't all come apart before your book gets published."

In American politics there are many times when a

man like Ford needs a man like Hartmann. Somebody has to be devil's advocate and worry about the what-ifs; somebody has to know where political skeletons are buried and where the traps, tigers and dangers are lurking.

Winter-Berger, author of the book attacking Ford, he felt, had been a potential trap but not because the man had eeled his way into the status of a tolerated guest in Ford's office. ("Ford never put his finger in the fire," Hartmann noted.) No, rather because Winter-Berger also had eeled his way into the office of aging House Speaker John McCormack, where corruption existed under the Democratic Speaker's nose. Winter-Berger, Hartmann said, spent much more time in the Speaker's office than in Ford's and must have known some of "the dirt" that was going on. This, Hartmann suspected, Winter-Berger peddled to Ford as the price of admission. Ford as Minority Leader for Republicans would understandably want to know what was going on.

"I think our office was an insurance policy in Winter-Berger's mind," Hartmann declared. "He heard the Attorney General's office in New York was after him and [Nathan] Voloshen; he wanted to build a sanctuary."

If this diagnosis were correct, Hartmann said further, he would still doubt that Ford had ever told anyone else any "dirt" that Winter-Berger might have provided him. But he marveled that Ford tolerated Winter-Berger so long, even though when Ford became convinced Winter-Berger had deceived and used him, "he cut off his water just like that."

Just the opposite kind of man was Paul Miltich, the veteran press secretary Ford took with him to the Old Executive Offices. Miltich, fifty-four, had been Ford's press secretary since 1966, coming from the ranks of newsmen as Hartmann had. Miltich was originally from Minnesota. An honors scholar in literature and languages, he went on to become a schoolteacher, but his career was quickly interrupted by World War II. After four years in the Army and a discharge with the rank of corporal, Miltich went to Saginaw, Michigan, where he started as a reporter and music critic. He became assistant city editor of the Saginaw *News,* and in 1957 went to Booth Newspapers' Washington bureau, where he met Ford. There was more than a bit of the Calvinist in Miltich: He did not believe in compromise with facts. Once, when his review of a local orchestral concert had been as rough as sandpaper, his editors on the Saginaw *News* had asked him to consider that it was "our own Saginaw production." Miltich said there could be no compromise with the difference between good music and bad music. The editors could tear up his review if they wished, but he would not write a lie. The Saginaw *News* published it as written.

Miltich had covered the events up to and including Ford's elevation to House Minority Leader in 1965. When Ford needed a press secretary, it was he who initiated conversations with Miltich about taking the job. At first Miltich doubted he belonged in partisan politics, but Ford asked him to consider it for a week. He offered the job again, setting forth only one requirement or warning: "In this office we work hard, we work long hours." Miltich decided to go with Ford.

Washington news media enjoyed reporting the fact —and it was fact—that Hartmann and Miltich did not get along very well, that each had his own view and therefore gave Ford differing counsel. Hartmann was conservative, Miltich a political moderate. Hartmann was full of ambition for Ford, Miltich constrained by an ethic. It was in the Ford style to have differing philosophies represented on his staff.

Another influence on Ford was President Nixon himself. He saw the President frequently, at times almost daily. Shortly after New Year's day of 1974, they had a long talk—alone. During this meeting the President outlined Ford's role as Vice President as he had planned it, and Ford said he came away more than satisfied with what amounted to his marching orders. He never pretended he was not subordinate to the boss; Ford said when he had something to say, the President listened to him. And they continued to meet and talk.

Nevertheless, Ford needed a large staff, and it was characteristic of him that one new addition would be L. William Seidman of Grand Rapids, head of the national accounting firm and a longtime friend. A lawyer and an accountant, Seidman was knowledgeable in business, economics, and foreign trade—a valuable "research person." And, incidentally, one of billionaire J. Paul Getty's tax accountants.

With Ford, as always, was his personal assistant, Mildred Leonard. The *Congressional Quarterly* noted tersely that she had been his congressional executive secretary twenty-two years. Those few words carry a world of meaning in Washington palace politics. They meant she knew almost as much as Ford knew about the past, present and future—Ford's Rose Mary Woods, who would never have to worry about what she did or did not do with a tape recording.

Dorothy Hessler, Ford's personal secretary since 1967, continued in that function. Nancy Howe became an assistant and social secretary to Mrs. Ford.

The complement of military aides was sharp as tacks and polite as pie in the civilian clothing they never could quite get accustomed to: Army Major General John M. Dunn, forty-seven, senior aide; Navy Commander Howard J. Kerr, thirty-four; and Marine Lieutenant Colonel America A. Sardo, forty-three, and a sizable detail of Secret Service agents guarding the body of the Vice President and his home.

General Dunn with Walter L. Mote, who remained as assistant to the presiding officer of the Senate, were the only holdovers from the large staff of former Vice President Agnew. Both were technicians who had done specialized jobs for the vice-presidential office rather than for Agnew personally. All of Agnew's staff of more than sixty got suitable jobs elsewhere; only two, and these nonpolitical, were taken on by Ford.

Ironically there was a problem in getting enough good secretaries, typists, clerks, the foot soldiers of any government. For a reason.

"The secretaries' grapevine in this town knows that Ford's office staff works long hours," Hartmann explained. "That we work Saturdays. And we could recruit some of the real professionals, the war-horses who work for Congressmen, who like politics, but that's something you just don't do. Not when you've got to lobby Congress and get along with its members. You can seduce a Congressman's wife, maybe, but don't ever hire away from him a good secretary. It's forbidden."

A visit to the Vice President's offices on a Saturday was like a late-night television mystery movie. The lights in the miles of long corridors were cut to a very few dim lamps (the energy crisis was on); most of the offices were locked and dark. But on the second floor, where the Vice President worked, Ford was very much in residence and so was his staff, trying to

43

get coordinated, cope with the flood of mail, the innumerable telephone calls, the shaping of a bureaucracy-nucleus capable of efficient function, capable of government. Everyone was aware of a startling political fact: Should the President fall one way or another, this was the staff that would move into the White House with new President Ford. They would be so much more important it was frightening for all to contemplate. Hence, perhaps, the frets of a Miltich, the qualms of a Hartmann, and the haunting thought: Is history changing faster than the mind can cope with it?

5 Dad Thought Character Began with Rules

Michigan became a territory in 1813, thanks to the strategic importance of Detroit and easy access via Lake Erie.

When the Erie Canal was built, it opened the upper Midwest to settlers and by 1837 the population was big enough for Michigan to become a state. In 1848 the first territorial Governor, Lewis Cass, was the unsuccessful Democratic candidate for President. Since that year many Michigan politicians nursed a hope that another child of Michigan would try and succeed. In 1974 Jerry Ford appeared closer than any other. At least he was Michigan's first Vice President.

Ford was born July 14, 1913, in Omaha, Nebraska, to Dorothy (née Gardner) King, wife of Leslie King, a Montana wool trader. When Jerry was two, his parents were divorced, and Mrs. King moved to Grand Rapids, where she had friends. There she met and married Gerald R. Ford, a paint salesman. Ford came to love Jerry and adopted him. Jerry knew this history, vaguely, but never thought about it much until one day when he was serving hamburgers at a restaurant across the street from South High School, a man entered and told him, "I'm your father." They had a brief visit and King left, still a stranger to Jerry, not to return again.

The overriding influence in his life as a child and as a mature man was his adoptive father. In all but the physical sense the elder Ford was Jerry's father. And after the parents died in the 1960's the heritage they gave him still guided Jerry Ford.

Life with Dad and Mother Ford had its burdens, but it was seldom dull.

Gerald R. Ford, Sr., a strong, self-made and very inner-directed man, had his life enlivened with four boys far enough apart in age to span a generation.

Dad was the absolute, final authority in the Ford family, an informal autocrat of the dinner table. So much of the Ford family life centered around that dinner table. It was a big, oval, solid mahogany table made at the old Berkey & Gay Furniture Company factory in downtown Grand Rapids. The Ford boys came to know the table intimately because one of Dad Ford's disciplines was "finish your plate." If not, it was sit there until you did, or bedtime, whichever came first.

Dad asked only three things of his one adopted and three natural sons: that they work hard to make something of themselves, speak the truth, and come to dinner on time.

The only instance of physical punishment the Ford brothers remember was when, in Dick's words, "Tom came to dinner late with an excuse that wasn't acceptable, and Dad broke a ruler over the seat of his britches." They didn't count a spoon thwacked on a careless elbow on the table—which was another of the older Ford's disciplines. In larger matters he helped them to make something of themselves, and his son Richard swears that Dad Ford actually guided them into their professions.

"He had an experience with the legal profession, sometime, somehow," said Dick. "An unhappy one. And Jerry became a lawyer, I am convinced, because of Dad's direction. I know in my own case I went to the University of Michigan to study chemical engineering because Dad thought it would be smart to have one in a family that made its living from a paint business. I believe he led Tom, and I'm sure Jim is an optometrist today because Dad urged him into it."

The other brothers weren't so sure about this and James, who became a successful optometrist and father of four fine children himself, simply didn't think it happened that way.

That was natural. The four Ford boys were different enough in age that each saw his own life in relation to the family in a different light. What they all agreed on is what kind of man their father was. The finest man who ever came down the pike, worthy of respect and emulation, fair and firm, but above all honest.

One time, as all family jokes begin, Dad saw a problem developing. Dick was becoming a good athlete in his late teens, and his ego was growing with his prowess. He became very interested in winning, whether it was tennis, golf, football or whatever. His drive to win was growing out of proportion.

When Jerry, Jr., came home on vacation from his job coaching football at Yale, Dad tried to engineer something. He privately urged Jerry, Jr., to take Dick out for a round of golf and, "as the hero of the family," the story goes, give Dick an elder-brotherly talk about sportsmanship, playing the game for its own sake, etc., etc. Jerry did, and over the span of sixteen holes of golf felt he was making progress. After all, he coached football at Yale and was in his twenties; Dick, in his mid-teens, looked up to Jerry.

On the seventeenth tee Jerry himself had a problem. He couldn't hit the ball. Stroke one dribbled it a few feet from the sand tee used in those days. Stroke two was a clean whiff. Stroke three was a ninety-degree slice. But number four found its mark: Jerry wrapped his driver around the sandbox.

He realized instantly what he had done, and turned slowly to face his younger brother. Dick was doubled up with mirth. Jerry began to laugh and they both howled. "See what I mean?" Jerry demanded between gasps. "Nobody can win all the time." Dad's strategy came out all right and the incident became one of the family's favorite jokes—within the family.

Then there's the family story of "The Night Jerry, Jr., Burned Up His Car." Much family history is dated by whether it came before or after that night in 1930.

The family had moved to East Grand Rapids the previous summer, but Jerry wanted to complete high school at South High and got school-board permission to spend his senior year there. He was all-city football center that fall for the third year in a row and for the first time made the all-state high school football team. He also won a movie theater's promotional contest as "most popular high school senior." The prize was a trip to Washington and that's how Jerry, Jr., first saw Washington, D.C. It was something like the Year of Jerry in the Grand Rapids area that winter. Except for the weather and the frailties of his 1922 Model T.

It was miles from the new Ford home to South High, and Jerry had spent seventy-five dollars of his summer earnings to buy the secondhand car to be able to commute. The first really cold night of winter he did what many Model-T owners did—put a blanket over the front. But he didn't throw it over radiator and hood, he raised the sides and put the blanket over the engine, under the hood.

Old-timers will remember that a Model-T engine

built up a reservoir of heat in a few miles of driving, especially if the weather was cold and the car's radiator system was crotchety. Within a few minutes after Jerry had entered the house Tom looked out the window and saw a cloud of smoke billowing up from the hood of the Model T and neighbors running toward the Ford home. The fire department was called. Buckets of water were brought. But the Model T was too far gone in flames. It burned to a shell in the driveway.

"Don't feel too bad, son," said Dad Ford. "I'm sure so-and-so can do something about this." He referred to a family friend and insurance agent he had recommended Jerry consult about insurance for the car.

"I didn't take out any insurance," Jerry confessed, tears welling in his eyes.

It was a strained supper that night because Jerry was a pedestrian again and as hurt as an eighteen-year-old can be over totaling out his first auto. It was a big enough catastrophe that Tom, at thirteen, and Dick, at nine, felt no desire to laugh. Jim, four, must have sensed calamity, but his memory years later was only "lots of smoke and fire."

The rest of the school year Jerry stoically rode the bus downtown and transferred to the South Division line, a three-quarter-hour trip each way and more in snowy weather. He spent the time studying.

Despite the tragedy with the Ford car, the elder Ford did not hesitate to use the public confidence in the name Ford to help him in the paint business. And Jerry, Jr., until he became Minority Leader and qualified for the standard chauffeured Cadillac always said, "What other kind of car would I drive?"

Jerry's father and mother were active in community affairs as far back as their sons can remember. Dad Ford articulated it at the dinner table, where conversation was not infrequently his explanation of a political situation or movement, a civic need or improvement plan. He was a charter director of one of the earliest programs of help for ghetto youth. It started with a recreation house in the highest-crime-rate area of Grand Rapids, near the point where the Negro quarter verged into the Italian quarter, and later as a summer camp for poor youths at the outskirts of the city. The project received free paint and other help from the Ford Paint Company, including the elder Ford's active participation.

He and his sons were doers, not thinkers; achievers, not critics or analysts. There were not many books in the Ford home, all agree.

At times Mrs. Ford must have felt swamped in masculinity but she, like most American women who reared families in the 1920's or 1930's, felt her family duty had first priority. She still had time left for her own social and community projects: the local symphony and musical programs, Grace Episcopal Church programs and activities including fundraising for charity. (She was outraged once when a family of much greater means than theirs contributed not a home-baked cake or bread to a charity sale, but two cans of store-bought beans.)

Mrs. Ella Koeze, a family friend, recalled that although Dorothy Ford's health was not good, she was nevertheless "vivacious, effervescent, fun to be with." She was active in church work, a gardener and collector of antiques. "She was an expert at making caramel candy, and at Christmastime the Ford living room was like an old-fashioned Christmas card because she filled it with gifts of cookies, candy, dolls and handmade outfits of doll clothing, all stacked around the tree—gifts for friends and friends' children as well as for her own family. Going to visit the

Fords was a happy part of our Christmas ritual," Mrs. Koeze related. She added that although some friends later said Jerry, Jr., resembled his adoptive father, it was not so. "His features were the image of his mother's."

Mrs. Ford was known to say on occasion that "if Dad would give as much time to the paint business as to public affairs, we'd be rich."

Nevertheless, for a man who had dropped out of high school in the tenth grade, Ford, Sr., was no slouch at business. He early went into business for himself and in the autumn of 1929 formed a corporation with an associate named C. L. Schumann—Dr. Schumann, no less, a chemical engineer at a time when doctors of science were scarce in Grand Rapids and chemical engineers virtually unknown. It was a town of master carpenters, cabinetmakers, and many Dutch painters and painting contractors certified as journeymen capable of the finest house painting, sign painting and billboard pictures. In Grand Rapids at that time about the only things that weren't made of wood and in need of frequent painting were city hall, Kent County courthouse, and the Fox Company brewery, which was like a Gothic stone castle atop Michigan Hill.

Ford, Sr., and Dr. Schumann held 51 percent of the corporation stock and later events made it possible to buy an even bigger share of the ownership. The first factory building was built on the old West Side of Grand Rapids (and was still standing in 1974). The paint manufacturing business was originally aimed at the Dutch painting contractors, but Ford would just as readily sell a pint of enamel at retail to anyone who walked in the door.

The factory started up just three weeks before the stock-market crash, and it was rough sledding from the very first. Later came the "bank holiday," a euphemism for the loss of most savings accounts and business checking accounts.

Within two days after the banks had closed Ford received a telegram from the Dupont Company, telling him to keep on ordering materials for paint manufacture; both parties could worry about payment later. "We'll work something out" was the phrase in the telegram.

Dad Ford was encouraged and essayed to "work something out" with his plant force of ten persons. He had no business bank account or money of his own, and his employees had only what was left in their pockets from last week's paycheck.

He could see a modicum of cash trickling in weekly and did some simple arithmetic. Then he went into the plant with his plan. "We can give you five dollars a week to buy groceries and fuel and keep going," he told his employees. "I plan to give myself the same amount in cash. When things get better, we will pay you back the difference between the five dollars and your normal pay, however long it takes." The employees stayed with Ford and ultimately were paid in full.

Later, the Ford Paint and Varnish Company never had trouble recruiting reliable workers. One might not get rich, but it was like joining a family to go to work for Ford, or in later years for his sons Tom or Dick.

With the onset of the Depression the oldest three sons quickly learned how paint was made and spent summers working in the factory. Tom Ford remembers the hard years in the early 1930's: "We had paint and enamel; we didn't have much money to buy other supplies. Now, one of the jobs is pasting labels on cans after they are filled, and I remember a time we simply had no paste. So we opened a big old Dun & Bradstreet business-rating book—who needed that in the Depression?—and set a paint can on it. Then we painted the can with varnish instead of paste and put on the label. After each can you'd turn the page of Dun & Bradstreet to get rid of the overflow varnish, set a new can on and start over."

Therein lies another "Jerry, Jr., joke." A paint-factory worker got lots of paint on his hands and frequently had to wipe his hands on a pants leg. Paint makers had to change pants after quitting work. Jerry, Jr., wore shorts in warm summer weather but still wiped paint off on his legs. The family joke went that he cleaned the accumulated paint off his legs every Friday.

What with hard work in the paint factory, restaurant kitchens or whatever way a Ford son earned a dollar, appetites were healthy. The family's tastes were simple—it was meat-potatoes-vegetables-bread at dinner—and food prices were almost incredibly low in those days. But even so Ford, Sr., believed in frugality. Once he complained about the amount of money Mrs. Ford needed to finance meals for a family weekend at their cottage on Lake Michigan, plus a guest or two of the boys, the hired housegirl, and family friends who dropped in and stayed to eat.

"Very well," said Mrs. Ford. "This coming week you buy the groceries and bring them when you drive over to the cottage Friday night." (She herself spent much of the summer at the cottage in the late 1930's.)

Ford did so. In the meat category alone he brought twenty-seven pounds of good-quality stuff. In all he spent much more than Mrs. Ford would have and never voiced a criticism again.

In the early 1930's it was necessary for Jerry to

work, first at the small restaurant across the street from South High School and then waiting fraternity-house tables at the University of Michigan. It was the "Deke" house, and he eventually became house manager and a member of the fraternity.

After graduation from the University of Michigan he was offered a job as assistant football and boxing coach at Yale, and—lacking funds to enter the University of Michigan law school as he had hoped—he saw it as a ticket to a law degree. As was usually the case when he had an important decision to make, he talked it over with his father.

Ford, Sr., argued that there was little future in football coaching. Sooner or later your team had a losing season—as Jerry well knew by 1936—but Jerry argued it would be only temporary and there was a good law school right at Yale and another nearby at Columbia University in New York. He took the Yale job.

Like Jerry, Ford, Sr., was also big. He was, in his mature years, six feet one inch tall and weighed 200 pounds. Through his middle and old age he suffered constantly from stomach ulcers and associated disorders, which were not so easily treated then as now. Often when the older Ford boys came home at night from a party or date, Ford would still be up, in the living room—not to keep track of their hours but because he simply could not sleep from discomfort.

Mrs. Ford was overweight and suffered high blood pressure, which occasionally sent her to bed or to the hospital. And in the 1940's she had a then-rare operation at University of Michigan hospital to correct a back nerve problem. Fortunately for her, household help was easy to get when the sons were in grade school and dirtying a mountain of dishes and clothing every day. Room, board and a few dollars a week were all the help cost, with many a farmgirl happy to take the job, learn city ways and possibly find a husband. Tom remembers one summer when a rural schoolteacher accompanied his mother to the cottage at no wage whatsoever, just to spend a summer on the shore of Lake Michigan.

After the first, worst impact of the Depression the Fords became comfortable, but not well-to-do. Early in the 1930's Dad and Mother Ford had moved from Grand Rapids' old section into East Grand Rapids, a middle-class residential suburb noted for its good school system. Many in Grand Rapids "moved up" that way, as their fortunes enabled them to. Ford had had to lose the first house he bought in East Grand Rapids to which they moved in 1929, because the mortgage holder would not renegotiate the size of payments after the onset of the Depression. He simply forfeited his down payment and started buying another house, on easier mortgage terms. There was nothing dishonorable about this in Grand Rapids in the early 1930's, or most other cities for that matter.

In business Ford practiced what he preached—"a man's word is his bond" and "if a thing is worth doing, it's worth doing well." Paying one's debts, abstaining from liquor, raising a fine family, contributing to the community welfare and giving one's children a good name constituted success in the community where Jerry Ford, Jr., grew up. When his father died, Grace Episcopal Church was packed to standing-room-only for his funeral, something that had never happened before in the church's history.

6 To End as a Man

Football was one of the biggest influences on Ford's life. It brought him to public attention as a teen-ager, it was a ticket to a university education and a law degree. It enhanced his courtship of Betty Bloomer, who studied under famous dancer and choreographer Martha Graham and believed, as Jerry did, in physical grace and fitness.

Football was much more important in Grand Rapids when Jerry Ford was growing up than it is today. There were fewer competing attractions, far fewer. No television, for one; not many students had autos available to them; social life for many was whatever one did after the Saturday afternoon football game. School-district boundaries were fixed on a city region basis, and there was no such thing as cross-busing; rivalry between high schools was high-spirited and fueled by neighborhood pride.

When Jerry Ford played football for South High School, the coach was Clifford Gettings, a very big man and a very dignified man. A fine university athlete in his youth, Gettings was totally devoted to football and successful at putting together winning teams. Many said he should have been coaching at university level. He lived to win and did not hesitate on the practice field to kick his players in the rear when they didn't try hard enough. If the player or his parents didn't like it, the boy could turn in his suit. It is not recorded that anyone ever made a federal case out of what today would be manifest brutality and grounds for dismissal of a faculty member. (Gerald Ford, Sr., once told the principal of another high school, who had put his son Tom on report, "Any punishment you choose, I will double when he gets home.")

Gettings determined that playing center was Jerry's forte. In those days there were more long snaps from center to backfield; the quarterback standing with his hands under the center's rump for a handoff or quarterback sneak was not so common. Thus, the center did a good deal of what amounted to passing the football from upside-down position. Strength of arm and accuracy were necessary, as well as the stamina to bear up under the opponent center's body hitting a split second after the ball moved. Jerry was named all-city center three years in a row playing for South.

Unlike many high school athletes Jerry was not gregarious or outgoing, a school contemporary recalled. He didn't cavort or joke or give trouble to teachers. Even then he was all business. Unlike most high school students of the day, he wore a suit and tie most of the time instead of the casual shirt, slacks and sweater that were so common.

He sought good grades and got them and spent little time with girls. One girl, who was in a junior-year American history class with Jerry, recalls he paid attention to her for a special reason. "Jerry and I were the best pupils in the class," recalled Virginia Berry, then a fifteen-year-old sophomore taking extra courses. "Our teacher gave weekly exams and the way it went was one week I would get a ninety-six and Jerry a ninety-three, next week he'd get a ninety-seven and I'd get a ninety-four. I sat in the back of the room and Jerry up front, and every time exams were returned he would come back to ask what my grade was. He didn't resent it if I got a better grade, he was just checking. We both got A's in that subject, the only two in the class.

"Jerry was big and handsome and two years older. And I had a problem. My father, who, as it happened, was athletic director at Union High, wouldn't let me date because I was only fifteen. I had boyfriends—we used to go across the street to the restaurant at lunchtime and dance to the jukebox, but you never saw Jerry there, of course.

"Well, I got this idea if I could only get Jerry out to my house, Dad would be impressed by him as an example of South High boys and let me date. So I tried to get Jerry to visit my home. No success: He never would come. I got the impression of a fellow with the mind of a child in a man's body, a big St. Bernard."

Coach Gettings urged Jerry to attend the University of Michigan and was helpful in the transition from high school to the big university in 1931. He was as popular at the university as he had been in high school. But the football situation was different.

"Where's your black player?" the Georgia Tech lineman taunted, in one of football history's most ill-advised japes. Three plays later he went off the field on a stretcher, to play no more against the University of Michigan that day. He had been hit simultaneously by Jerry Ford and guard William Borgmann.

The black player was Willis F. Ward, Michigan end and also a track star, an outstanding athlete by anybody's standards, above or below the Mason-Dixon line. He was listening to the game over radio because Georgia Tech had vowed not to take the field if Michigan's black player did.

Ward, almost thirty years later, put part of the

blame on Fielding Yost, then the University of Michigan athletic director, for knuckling under to the Georgia Tech ultimatum.

"It was the third game of the 1934 season, and dropping me from the lineup for racist reasons did something to team morale," he related. "We just never got together as a close-knit team after that. And I didn't play that day because Coach Harry Kipke was told not to put me in uniform. The administration wasn't eager to have blacks on the team anyway. Kipke finally got enough alumni support to put me on the varsity, and I was the first black to play a full three years of varsity football for Michigan."

Ford had agonized the night before and almost decided not to suit up or go on the field himself. He had phoned his father in Grand Rapids to tell him about the situation and ask his advice.

"This is one you'll have to decide for yourself, son," the elder Ford told him.

One reason Ford decided to play was that it was at best a scratched-together Michigan team. The loss of a good lineman might mean defeat. All through 1932 and 1933 they had been undefeated, Big Ten champions. Then a mass graduation of varsity players left Kipke with three regular starters and a mob of eager second-stringers.

The year never got any better after the Georgia Tech game, which Michigan won 9-2. That year Minnesota defeated Michigan 34-0, the first time Minnesota had even scored on Michigan since 1929, and the first Minnesota victory against anybody since 1929.

Ford put his feelings about his football years into words twenty-five years later when he was named to one of *Sports Illustrated*'s silver-anniversary all-America roster of football players. "Thanks to my football experience, I know the value of team play," said Jerry. "It is, I believe, one of the most important lessons to be learned and practiced in our lives. You learn to accept discipline. My experiences in games like that with Minnesota helped me many times to face a tough situation in World War II or, in the rough-and-tumble of politics, to take action and make every effort possible despite adverse odds."

Football in the early 1930's was quite different from today, Ward pointed out in his reminiscences. "You had to be a two-way, sixty-minute player. Coaches didn't have unlimited substitutions. If you got hurt, then you were substituted. The ball was somewhat bigger and rounder. You didn't pass as much. And the center had to think in those days. On defense he was a linebacker or what we called 'roving center.' On offense he had to know where to pass the ball, do it accurately and with exact timing. Jerry wasn't heavy, he was quick," Ward recalled.

Ward said Jerry never told him he had considered refusing to take the field against Georgia Tech, but, "it was just like Jerry. During orientation week he walked up to me on the campus, introduced himself and we were friends all the way through Michigan. He was a standout. In my mind he was a decent guy."

Ward said he was unhappy with criticism from some quarters that Jerry was a mediocrity, an intellectual lightweight, a blindly loyal supporter of President Nixon. "He was a solid B student at one of the five best universities in the country," Ward noted. "He played a position in football where you have to think. He coached football and won a law degree at Yale. He led his political party in the House of Representatives. What more do they want of a guy? And as for loyalty, this country could stand some of that. Of children toward their parents, for instance."

The last comment may stem from Ward's experience as probate judge in Wayne County, which includes Detroit.

Ward said he regretted that "Jerry didn't develop as a football player the way he could have." Ford didn't get to start at center until the 1934 season when he was named the team's most valuable player. For the first two years he was second-string center behind all-American Chuck Bernard.

The captain of the 1933 championship team, Stanley Fay, later a Detroit-area real estate agent, recalled Jerry as "a player who had no fear, and a smart guy too. I was always a little jealous of him because he was a lot better student than I was," Fay said. (Ford received his B.A. in liberal arts with a B average. The courses in which he earned A's were Money and Credit, European History from the Decline of Rome to 1648, Labor, and American Government.)

Bennie Oosterbaan, all-American end at Michigan in the 1920's and assistant coach when Jerry played, later termed Jerry "a leader, mostly by example. In his early days he was a quiet person but an enthusiastic worker."

Even after graduation from Michigan Jerry Ford was not done with football. He played in the 1935 Shrine East-West game, and then came an opportunity Jerry didn't feel he could refuse, even if it meant going against his father's advice. Yale's football coach, Raymond "Ducky" Pond, was a friend of Michigan's Kipke and came to Ann Arbor to visit in the summer of 1935. He needed an assistant to handle the freshman football squad and also coach boxing, a full-time salaried position. Pond asked Kipke if he would recommend anyone among his graduating varsity players for the job. Kipke named three, including

61

Jerry Ford. It turned out the other two players were returning home to family businesses and were not interested in coaching, so the job went to Ford.

When asked how he handled the boxing part of his duties, Jerry confessed that as soon as he was picked to go to work in September of 1935, he began taking lessons from Stanley Levandoski, a former amateur boxing champion. "Then," Jerry said, "at Yale I boxed the lightweights and coached the heavyweights."

Ford was proud later that his academic record at Yale from 1935 to 1941 was as good as his record at the University of Michigan: B average. Ford, many years later, said he had persuaded the Yale law school faculty members to let him take courses part-time on a trial basis: "If I got good grades, I could continue; if not, I would quit." The dean had warned him that more than two-thirds of the students in the law school were Phi Beta Kappa scholars. Obviously the mandarins of the law were dubious about the intellectual capacities of this young athlete from Michigan. But they let him try. After he carried half a normal academic load with fair grades in his first year of coaching boxing and teaching the junior varsity to block and tackle, he was allowed to continue.

Life was not all grind, grunt and sweat at Yale. Ford began to expand his social life, sharing a bachelor apartment with a basketball coach and often visiting New York on Saturday night to socialize.

One of Ford's early girlfriends was Phyllis Brown, a student at Connecticut College for Women. On Jerry's part it was almost a steady-date situation for four and a half years. "I almost married that girl," Ford recalled. He took her home to Michigan to meet the folks, play tennis and golf and enjoy a summer respite at the cottage on Lake Michigan. It was a happy association based as much on love of sports and a good time as anything. And it led to Ford's first business investment—in the modeling business.

After leaving college, Phyllis had become a Powers model in New York. She met Harry Conover, a male model and she wrote to Jerry, "You and he ought to go into business with each other; there's room for another agency." Ford agreed to put up $1,000 cash as the capital investment, enough to rent an office and hang out a sign; Conover was to furnish the knowledge, the expertise in esthetics and the marketing of bodily grace and charm. They formed a simple partnership under law and went into business.

The modeling business succeeded all right. And in March, 1940, Jerry himself took a fling at modeling for *Look* magazine. He and Phyllis went to New England in sports outfits and ski clothing, caracoling in the winter snow before the camera. The article in *Look* was about beautiful young people who pursued outdoor sports. Of the twenty-one photo illustrations, Ford appeared in seventeen—looking very good, indeed. A beautiful couple. Jerry always was photogenic.

The Conover agency succeeded, but Jerry never worked at running any part of it. He was to get a percentage of the profits but was soon far removed from New York. He said much later, "Expenses must have been very high because I didn't receive what I thought I might be entitled to."

He obtained the services of a New York attorney who arranged to cash Jerry out of the business and return his investment. Whether this had anything to do with the fact Jerry never went back East to resume a relationship with Phyllis or Conover is not known. She married—several times. They met in the early 1970's when Jerry was on a speaking trip to Nevada.

Jerry wasn't sure if Phyllis was with husband number two or number three at the time, but recalls them as "charming and cordial" to him, and wishing him well.

7 The War Years

Ford was admitted to the Michigan bar in June of 1941, and he and a friend, Philip Buchen, launched their infant law firm. Ford set out to specialize in labor cases and Buchen in corporation law. Within six months the Japanese attack on the American Navy at Pearl Harbor had canceled their plan indefinitely.

Ford went into uniform April 20, 1942, and his service record notes it was as "volunteer, special service (deck duties)." He was commissioned directly as an ensign under what was nicknamed "the Tunney fish program," for Gene Tunney, former Navy man and heavyweight boxing champion of the world. The program was aimed at fast recruitment of athletes to form a cadre of physical-training instructors who would whip many thousands of Navy recruits into good physical condition as quickly as possible. Ford was given indoctrination and navigation training at Annapolis.

In six weeks he was sent to Chapel Hill, North Carolina, where he spent a year giving physical training to Navy aviation cadets—and writing letters through channels volunteering for sea duty. Jockstrapping wasn't enough of a war effort for Jerry Ford. He was twenty-eight at the time of the Pearl Harbor attack and like many others personally wanted to do something about it. The fastest way to meet the Japanese was in the Navy, and that's where he went. But Chapel Hill was cushy shore duty; he even had the company of an old chum from South High School, track coach Danny Rose, who had entered the Navy under the same athletic program.

It took twelve months before Ford's persistence won assignment to Norfolk Navy station for brief gunnery training; then on to Camden, New Jersey, where the new light aircraft carrier USS *Monterey* was being readied for sea trials and assignment to the Pacific. He was in the original crew as physical-training director and assistant navigation officer. After a shakedown cruise and preliminary training—in which Jerry Ford and his shipmates learned the uses of forty-millimeter antiaircraft cannon, head-winds for aircraft landings, helmets as protection against flying metal splinters and the Mae West lifejacket in case worse came to worst—the ship headed for the Pacific.

One day in mid-December, 1944, it almost came to the worst. The *Monterey* was with the third fleet of Admiral William "Bull" Halsey in the South Pacific when the fleet was hit by a typhoon. Winds of one hundred miles an hour and more capsized three destroyers and drowned their crews. The *Monterey* survived but took serious damage when aircraft on the hangar deck crashed against each other during steep rolls and touched off gasoline fires. Flying wreckage punctured ventilator tubes; smoke that could not be blown out of the engine rooms smothered the ship's boilers and asphyxiated three men. The rest of the engine-room crew was overcome—the *Monterey* was wallowing helplessly in giant waves. General-stations call was sounded. Ford tried to get to his station on the bridge but didn't make it the first attempt. He stepped out on the heaving flight deck, lost his footing, slid across it "like a toboggan" and went right over the side—then dropped neatly into a catwalk a few feet down. He was unhurt but spent a moment before climbing back up on deck to wonder if the Ford luck was about to fail him. It didn't: He made station; the *Monterey* weathered the storm. Ford at war's end said it always was a lucky ship.

During the final phase of the war in the Pacific, the *Monterey* took part in every major naval battle. Among its combat engagements the official records list assaults on the Gilbert Islands, New Ireland, the Marshalls, Truk, Tinian-Saipan and Palau, the first and second battles of the Philippine Sea, raids on Wake Island, Formosa, Okinawa, the successful landing in the Philippines. Often under Japanese air attack, the *Monterey*'s good fortune held all the way, although a sister in its light-carrier class, the USS *Princeton,* was sunk.

Captain L. T. Hundt, the *Monterey*'s commanding officer, gave to the now Lieutenant Ford the best possible report in his officer's record file—a maximum of number four. The lowest Ford ever received from a superior officer (and this on shore duty or in training) was 3.7. Immediate superiors rated Ford as "excellent leader," "outstanding," "steady, reliable, resourceful," and "excellent organizer."

One Captain Harry E. Sears stated for the Navy's records that Ford was "at his best in situations dealing directly with people because he commanded the respect of all with whom he came in contact."

With performance ratings like that Ford might well have had a future in the Navy, but he was eager to return to Grand Rapids. He was discharged from active duty into the Navy reserves with the rank of lieutenant commander, ten battle stars on his victory ribbon. He returned to Grand Rapids at the end of 1945 with seventy days' accumulated paid leave.

Ford genuinely liked the Navy, all the services in fact, and was to have a long association with high officers of the armed forces during twenty-five years as a Congressman. But he was not a military careerist by nature. He said many years later he felt the Central Intelligence Agency was necessary because the nation had to have "an intelligence-gathering operation that is autonomous, independent of the armed forces." Nor did he seek opportunities to talk about his experiences in war. Ford always said later that the war convinced him to be "an internationalist." He believed isolationism had paved the way to the disastrous losses at Pearl Harbor. To Ford it was one of the most serious lessons in his training.

When Ford arrived home in time for Christmas of 1945, he was thirty-two years old. He had spent eight years playing football and six coaching it; he had lived ten years on university campuses; he had just finished a little less than four years in uniform during a world war; he had practiced law only six months. Like many who had spent some of the most impressionable years of their lives in war, he was very mature in some respects, almost naïve in others. But Jerry Ford was eager to get moving, to earn a living, relate to the community, be a part of something enduring. To start out, he moved in with his parents on Santa Cruz Drive in East Grand Rapids.

8 In the Valley of the Grand, by the Rapids

"Some say Jerry Ford is a square," a television commentator intoned on a special news background broadcast. "But perhaps he's just as simple and sturdy as Grand Rapids furniture."

Around "simple and sturdy" revolves a whole syndrome of myths that reveal the incurable romanticism of the "Eastern establishment news media." In the New York-Washington axis there are perhaps fifty or sixty influential major TV network commentators, syndicated columnists and political writers with the power to create and perpetuate myths. But they create romantic, not savage, myths.

The "simple, sturdy" or regional myth is common, and few newsmen working against deadlines can say they never fell for it. Many over the generations have helped embellish it; the regional myth goes this way: There is much that is good in American politics, but you have to get away from the strip of Atlantic coast between Long Island Sound and the Potomac River to find it. The farther you go, the simpler and sturdier (for which equate lovable and foursquare) the politicians get. Down Easters are craggy-featured politicians with rumpled suits (the old use-it-up, wear-it-out bit), but they are pawky men given to answering questions with aphorisms. Southerners are shrewd but sometimes rascally, speak in a drawl (variously described as syrupy, honey-coated, or thick), and they use the congressional seniority system to bring home to their districts plenty of pork in the form of dams, roads, military bases. Rogues maybe, but charming ones.

At the Pennsylvania-Ohio line, the Midwestern corn starts cropping up—and the crop gets cornier the farther west you go. Mayor Richard Daley could orate in unparsable sentences, and turn out a million voters to line a boulevard.

The mythical image of the politician changes subtly from bib-overall country to the plains and to Texas. This slight change in character accounts for the different myths about a Senator Everett McKinley Dirksen from Illinois and a ranching Senator Barry Goldwater from Arizona or a Lyndon Baines Johnson from Texas.

California baffled the myth makers because of its complexity, its little old ladies in tennis shoes who voted for Governor Ronald Reagan, its Chicanos roaring affection for the Kennedys, who in turn learned to shout *"viva la causa,"* whether the *causa* at the moment was grapes, lettuce or avocados. California is unexplainable, so let's get back to something simple and solid. Like Jerry Ford, Grand Rapids furniture, and Dutch burghers who started as immigrants in the furniture plant and whose first English words in the old days were, "I work by John Widdicomb a dollar a day." In nearby Holland, Michigan, there is a spring tulip festival, and even a Jerry Ford is not too dignified to put on wooden shoes and help Dutch matrons give the main street a symbolic scrubbing. With real soap and water and scrub brushes. How's that for a regional political ritual?

All very fine, but political life is not really that simple. Grand Rapids and West Michigan, even back

70

in 1946, when Jerry Ford came home from the war, formed a politically sophisticated metropolitan area where you could buy a murder contract on a state Senator who talked too much, juggle tax assessments to reward the faithful and punish enemies, or con the city commission into purchasing a moribund brewery from its worried stockholders.

Grand Rapids had established gambling joints, open all night long and selling liquor after legal hours. You could play poker, shoot craps or bet on horses. One downtown horse-race betting parlor operated at the same place for years with full knowledge of police and Western Union until the reformers demanded that it be raided. An after-hours establishment in the Negro quarter had a large neon sign out front for years.

There was a red-light district, and by senior year in high school many youths knew just where its boundaries were. Fittingly, most of the bordellos were along a street named Commerce Avenue, just south of downtown.

This was with the knowledge of the administration in city hall and of the police department. Both were proud that on the police force was a black police captain, Walter Coe. That, they thought, showed how progressive and tolerant Grand Rapids was—and how well-managed. Coe usually got a call within hours after a Chicago or Detroit black came to town for reasons other than promoting civic good. His information network pervaded the Negro quarter. Coe's methodology was simple: Warn the hood to get out of town if he hadn't had time to commit a felony, bust him hard and throw every charge possible at him if he had. This kept the rackets under local control, and also the revenues therefrom. Outside entrepreneurs learned to their sorrow it was a very clannish city. And discreet. Policemen going off duty at night walked the short block from headquarters to the back door of the Fox Brewery and drank all the free beer they wanted.

This was the kind of politics Jerry Ford and his backers wanted to change, but it didn't come easy.

Grand Rapids, second largest city in the auto state and old, as cities go in Michigan, had a colorful history going back to fur-trapping days, when two traders, Louis Campau and Lucius Lyons, fleeced Indians and white settlers alike to acquire what is now downtown Grand Rapids. The two men worked not in partnership but in competition. Because each owned about half the town, and neither would plan his holdings so streets would jibe at the boundary, downtown Grand Rapids today is askew to traffic.

The furniture makers, who imported Dutch immigrants by the boatload, learned a lesson from Lyons and Campau. They worked together and succeeded in keeping the auto industry and the industrial unions out of Grand Rapids until after World War II.

In this setting was a political machine that had run quite well for two decades. When Jerry Ford came home from the war, it was under attack but still the dominant political force. Republican, of course. There was no effective, enduring Democratic party in Michigan until after 1948.

At the controls of this machine was a gray eminence wearing a pince-nez: Frank D. McKay. McKay was a financier, banker, insurance broker, arranger of contracts with the state, and a boss of the old, established Republican party. A national committeeman, no less. Michigan was long a Republican state and McKay was long one of the party powers. His power was on the wane, but he was still the most formidable

72

pol in the western half of Michigan and had many friends at the state capital and in Detroit. Little happened in Michigan politics that McKay did not hear about, quickly.

Cock of the walk in city hall was George W. Welsh, a nimble-witted, silver-tongued demagogue who seemed always to know what the people wanted to hear and was crowning a long political career as Grand Rapids' mayor. Under McKay's sponsorship Welsh started political life as boy speaker of the state House of Representatives, then became boy lieutenant governor. In the 1920's he seemed to have a brilliant future, but in the 1930's he came home to run city hall and ultimately to fall out with McKay.

Also at the cutting edge of Grand Rapids politics was a classic ward heeler, a petty boss who worried about day-to-day pragmatics of running the city right: Jacob ("Jake" to everyone in Grand Rapids) Ryskamp, proprietor of a large downtown meat market. In between cutting good beef roasts at reasonable prices, Ryskamp was available in his back office to consult with a likely candidate for city commission, a contract seeker, a fellow politician with an unexpected money need. If you wanted good advice, a quick loan or an opinion on your own political future, Jake's back office was a good place to start. One might end talking with McKay in the McKay Tower, but Jake was a starting point.

McKay had various business subsidiaries: One sold tires to the state; another dealt in real estate; another in insurance. He was involved in high finance, too, and in the 1940's was indicted on a charge of conspiracy to make illegal profits from the bond financing for the Blue Water Bridge between Michigan and Canada at Port Huron. It was also said you couldn't sell so much as one road grader to the state highway department without the assent of the McKay machine. But McKay was never convicted of anything. Ryskamp supplemented his butcher-shop income with contracts to supply food for state institutions, and in other ways benefited from his broad knowledge of politics and people. The political reformers of the time claimed he was a bag man for the political machine—one who served as a collecting point for cash tribute. They never proved it.

The McKay machine functioned well during the war years; so did the lobbying and the fixing at Lansing, the capital. It was business as usual for the pols, and even better than usual because the public and the press had eyes riveted on the war news.

Then came one of those accidents of history that shake up the body politic. Michigan had its equivalent of a Watergate.

An obscure state Representative, William C. Stenson of Greenland, Michigan, began saying in speeches in his home district that he had found five hundred dollars cash stuffed into his overcoat pocket as it hung in the cloakroom outside the House chamber. Furthermore, he said he thought it came from a lobbyist.

A Detroit good-government group found a lot of special-interest legislation afloat and much questionable lobbying. There was a bill to fatten parimutuel horse-race profits and another to legalize greyhound dog racing. There was a bill to benefit naturopaths, a bill to allow bigger profits for small-loan companies. And there was a bill to allow branch banking—a goal of big Michigan banks for many years.

But the banks had a special difficulty; their lobbyists had to get many more votes than most lobbyists. A state constitutional provision required that any banking legislation must have a two-thirds majority vote in both House and Senate to pass.

Stenson believed some of the lobbyists were systematically buying votes in the legislature, and he so testified before the Carr-Sigler grand jury that was called to investigate the whole lobby mess. The grand jury spent tedious months taking testimony from many persons, including legislators. And strange things began to happen. An official of a Grand Rapids trucking company under grand-jury investigation, Harvey Bylenga, was killed when a train hit his car. State Senator Earl W. Munshaw of Grand Rapids was found in his auto, motor still running, in the family garage—dead of carbon-monoxide poisoning two days after he had testified to the grand jury.

A short time after Munshaw's death the state was electrified by a killing à la the Godfather. State Senator Warren G. Hooper of Albion testified before the grand jury. He was believed to have talked about McKay and others interested in banking legislation. Two days later, as he drove home from the capital, he was shot to death on a lonely southern Michigan road and his car was set afire.

In January, 1945, it appeared nobody's life was safe. The Carr-Sigler grand jury was hurriedly given $250,000, a big investigative staff, and public approval for an investigation that turned into a circus.

Circuit court judge and grand juror Leland W. Carr unleashed the flamboyant Kim Sigler to go full tilt at any target he might find. Sigler, a Barry County lawyer with a mane of prematurely white hair, on loan to the grand jury, became a real crusader.

Result? Many indictments but only four legislators convicted of graft; a number of lobbyists scorched and their effectiveness ruined; much of the questionable legislation stalled and dying on the legislative calendar as the year ended. There was a hue and cry after Frank D. McKay, who was popularly suspected of having been somewhere in the background of Senator Hooper's execution. One piece of gossip in Grand Rapids at the time had it that McKay had given a large sum of money to his lieutenants with instructions to "take care of" Hooper, by which he was supposed to have meant get Hooper out of the country. But the lieutenants had misunderstood the boss. . . . So went the gossip.

As a result of Sigler's investigations four men who had been serving time in Southern Michigan Prison at the time of the shooting were convicted of conspiracy to murder Hooper—but not of the actual murder. It was not explained at the trial, however, how one or more of them could have gotten out, done the shooting and then returned to the prison undetected. It was not until later that another scandal brought to light the fact that at the time of the Hooper murder it was not unusual for a con with money or friends in the right places to be given a brief sabbatical outside the walls—usually for a tryst with a girlfriend or a clandestine drinking party. Thus, there had been demonstrable opportunity there for a clever killing.

But it should be noted that Frank D. McKay was not the only rich and powerful man with an interest in the branch-banking bill and that many years of investigation and further study failed to dredge up any connection between McKay and the Hooper murder. What was significant was that many in Michigan believed the McKay organization capable of the deed.

On the other side in west Michigan politics there was an improbable group of reformers who set out very deliberately to break McKay's hold on the

Republican party and Grand Rapids government. Compared to McKay, they were amateurs, and no odds maker of the time would have given them much chance.

Organizer of this reform group was a dentist, W. B. VerMeulen, or "Doc," as friends called him. In the name of "the boys on the fighting fronts" he formed a political apparatus dubbed "the Home Front." He organized methodically, starting at the precinct level just as any professional pol would. He had the instincts of a demagogue and a ward heeler; he knew exactly what he was doing. He wanted to break McKay's political power, and he just happened to be on the right side of history.

Highly moralistic, VerMeulen might well have been dubbed God's angry man of Grand Rapids. He called McKay's works evil and blamed the community evils he found on McKay. All of them. It was a personal crusade, the crusade of a zealot. In 1944 Ver-Meulen had helped make Gerald Ford, Sr., county GOP chairman. VerMeulen had influence, but he lacked manpower. At the end of 1945 the manpower came streaming home, and he was in business.

Home Front activists in the public eye included Paul G. Goebel, a former University of Michigan football hero and proprietor of the leading Grand Rapids sporting-goods store—profitable because it sold so much athletic equipment to the city school system.

And there was John B. Martin, an attorney, a Rhodes scholar, and his ambitious wife. He was imbued with a most gentlemanly determination to contribute to the public good.

Ella Koeze, wife of a peanut-butter manufacturer, was another well-known figure in the Home Front. A political activist in the 1930's, Ella recalled one of her first experiences, "circulating petitions for the chosen slate and getting the standard ten-dollar bill from Frank McKay for doing it." She also recalled GOP convention delegates voting McKay's way after he had financed their travel, hotel and meals. When Doc VerMeulen organized the Home Front early in the 1940's, she was more than ready to join. She was a good friend of the Ford family, became county GOP vice-chairman and then served as Republican national committeewoman from 1960 to 1968.

John R. Stiles, scion of a reputable Grand Rapids family in the building-materials business, was a young Navy veteran, an idealist who had tried writing fiction after the war but soon shifted to politics and the Home Front.

There were others of the same genre, respected people who had never before engaged actively in politics—young attorneys, schoolteachers. The Home Front shrewdly recruited mothers and housewives with its pitch for clean government. The McKay machine had never truckled to women. It was an old-fashioned male-chauvinist outfit.

And there was Jerry Ford, whose fate it was to grow up in politically interesting times, in a community where public affairs were anything but simple. What he and other political reformers tried to do was restore simple honesty to public affairs. And like most reformers the first lesson they learned was you can bring all the honesty in the world to politics but you can't make it simple.

For instance, financier McKay had considerable real-estate holdings, including a large downtown bank building. He was personally interested, therefore, in property assessments. So were the Home Front reformers, who claimed the city-hall record in property assessing was one of light assessments for political and business cronies, higher assessments for ordinary, nonpolitical business firms and for opponents of the McKay-Welsh regime.

It had been considered a victory for the reform movement when, after the war, Frank Goebel, a brother of Paul Goebel, was appointed city assessor. Frank proceeded to do what he thought was an honest job in a fair way. But he bothered the wrong interests and Mayor Welsh fired him, with the blessing of a complacent city-commission majority. This spurred the reformers even more than the Hooper murder had. A recall movement against Welsh and three city commissioners who backed him was begun immediately.

It was launched in a very old-fashioned way with a torchlight parade and a mass rally of citizens at Grand Rapids' Fulton Park, in the middle of downtown and only a few blocks from city hall. Several thousands appeared. There were speeches by the Home Front leaders while activists like Jack Stiles roamed through the crowd chanting slogans such as "four must go." The crowd responded well and downtown Grand Rapids echoed with a roar that had not been heard since V-J Day. Welsh later called it a mob and blamed VerMeulen, Stiles and company for the worst kind of demagogy. "Lynch mob" were Welsh's words, and the truth is the Home Fronters did call for a political lynching, but in legal ways.

The recall movement, by statutory methods, was effective; it brought an overturn in the city-commission majority and the resignation of Mayor Welsh. A political opportunist named Stanley J. Davis became interim mayor by commission vote while the Home Fronters organized themselves behind Paul Goebel, who was elected mayor in a landslide at the next election. One of Mayor Goebel's first acts was not to reinstate his brother—that would have been impolitic—but to hire a professional city assessor from the East, who proceeded to raise a lot of property assessments, not just downtown but all over the city. Even some of the "silk-stocking bluebloods," as Welsh scornfully called the reformers, had been coasting on low tax assessments.

This was the setting in which Jerry Ford committed himself to public affairs and elective office. He certainly had no illusions about politics; but he did have ideals and goals. And ambition.

But Jerry Ford, when he sought his first term in Congress, had a long way to go. Michigan had a political colossus in Congress who cast a national shadow —Senator Arthur Vandenberg of Grand Rapids, one of the major architects of the United Nations. His conversion from isolationism to internationalism in the middle of World War II was a spectacular victory for the one-worlders. Vandenberg even had mild dreams of the presidential nomination at the 1948 Republican national convention, but his floor manager was Michigan Governor Kim Sigler, elected to the highest state office because of his dragon-slaying image. With a floor manager like Sigler he didn't need enemies, and Vandenberg never got off the ground as a presidential aspirant. Sigler, incidentally, was a one-termer. He kept muttering to reporters his suspicions about McKay, and he stepped on many other kinds of Republican toes. In 1948 the party leaders ditched him and allowed a young Democrat to be elected, G. Mennen "Soapy" Williams, heir to a shaving-soap fortune. The professional Republicans thought it worth a two-year sabbatical from the governor's office to get rid of Sigler. Williams served twelve consecutive years before retiring undefeated and reduced the Republican party to a second-rate power in Michigan. That was a lesson Jerry Ford never forgot. He never neglected his home base, never scorned a vote or ignored a constituent.

But in the halcyon years of 1946, 1947, 1948, few Republicans dreamed what the future would bring. They had most of the marbles and the biggest battles were between Republican factions over the marbles. At his debut in 1948, Jerry Ford was far below the likes of Senator Vandenberg and Frank D. McKay in the political pecking order. McKay did little when young Ford challenged incumbent Congressman Bartel J. Jonkman.

Jonkman was the kind of Grand Rapids citizen the television commentator must have had in mind when he talked about "simple, sturdy" politicians. A real Frisian stonehead, opponents were quick to tell the uninitiated. Frisian stonehead is the epithet, coined from an area of the Netherlands, that one Grand Rapids Dutchman used for another who was too stubborn to be tolerated even by other Dutchmen.

Like Vandenberg, Jonkman had gone into World War II an isolationist and had, with Vandenberg, voted against appropriations to modernize and enlarge the armed forces. This writer remembers, after joining the local National Guard regiment in 1936, a senior non-com pointing to a .75 mm cannon of World War I vintage coupled to an old truck and saying, "That's the kind of mechanization we get from those Dutch politicians of ours. They'd vote against a nickel if it was for the armed forces."

However, Vandenberg emerged from the war a father to the United Nations. Jonkman managed to come out neoisolationist. That's real stubbornness, and it made Jonkman very vulnerable. It didn't require much urging to get Jerry to run against Jonkman.

81

But the Home Fronters and reformers didn't take anything for granted, and Jerry waged an underdog's campaign. Jerry later said that in the first campaign he learned some things that were useful all through his political life; pitching hay was one of them.

9 Beginning

The Home Front Republican political organization of "Doc" VerMeulen was a handy incubator for ambition and talent. Many dreams were revealed and plans concocted over lunch at the Cherrie Inn, where the Home Fronters gathered.

One of the earliest plans was that Jerry Ford should run for Congress and John Martin for state Senate. If the revered Senator Vandenberg left his seat or died, somebody in the reform group—possibly Martin—would run for U.S. Senate. Lucky Jerry was the star of the dream's first stage and needed no urging to gird himself for a 1948 primary-election battle against incumbent Congressman Jonkman. He was eager to make hay and little knew he would soon be doing it literally, to great political advantage.

A story persisted all through Jerry's career that he and Martin both were interested in Congress in 1948 and actually flipped a coin to decide which man should run against Jonkman. Jerry certainly was grateful for Martin's support and showed it in important ways later on.

At thirty-five Jerry had the right amount of youth, the right amount of maturity, and an abundance of masculine handsomeness. He was eminently electable, and everyone knew it. But it remained to set up the right timing and establish Jerry's public image. There was no lack of support in the community, or of good advice.

"Doc" VerMeulen had a penchant for hurling charges at McKay that were hard to document with solid evidence. Night editors and lobster-trick reporters on the two daily newspapers were warned to beware of a VerMeulen blast at McKay just before deadline. Often as not it would be libelous.

Jerry Ford's first manifestation of political savvy was to remain aloof from the highly personal assault VerMeulen conducted against McKay for years. He had the full support of the Home Front organization without chowdering and marching with it.

Jerry's problems were twofold: Congressman Jonkman was the incumbent and his name and ancestry were Dutch. VerMeulen charged that Jonkman was a McKay man and therefore—in VerMeulen's bestiary —likely to have considerable money and sinister weapons at his command. McKay didn't even pay attention to the contest. He was frying bigger fish, including real-estate investments that eventually reached to the Miami Beach area.

Jerry Ford pondered the public mood and the ethnic composition of Kent and Ottawa Counties. Voters, he was sure, were ready for youthful zeal, honesty, and a platform of participating in world affairs. In short a war veteran who had seen the far reaches of the Pacific Ocean and knew the world didn't stop at America's shores.

But what kind of voters were they? In Grand Rapids the population was about half Dutch, perhaps one-quarter Polish, and the rest a melange of white Anglo-Saxon Protestants like Jerry, Italians, blacks, and Germans. The Dutch vote was all-important.

Jerry decided on two main campaign methods: going out on the street and into the countryside to shake the hand of every voter he could and drumming away at Jonkman with a challenge to personal debate on support of the United Nations, U.S. participation in international affairs, maintaining strong armed forces, and other national issues. He did not mention McKay.

It was an improvised campaign, corny and slam-bang at times. If a 4-H club held a milking contest, Jerry didn't mind visiting and having his picture taken at the production end of the cow. If there was a community festival in Cedar Springs, Jerry was glad to speak or be introduced from the speaker's platform.

He became the darling of Nina Babcock and Grace Hamilton, known throughout Kent County as "the Clipper Girls." They were two New Yorkers who had left the big city to buy the Cedar Springs *Clipper,* a small weekly newspaper, and enjoy the tempo of rural Midwest journalism. The *Clipper* supported Jerry's campaign enthusiastically.

Of course, he had his enemies. One time Jerry appeared at a Cedar Springs meeting. Coming out of the building he encountered none other than Frank D. McKay. The gray eminence, who seldom appeared in public in Grand Rapids, had taken the trouble to journey a few miles north to size up the young interloper.

"Hello, Mr. McKay, how are you, sir?" were Jerry's words.

McKay uttered just one sentence before departing: "I like your style, young man, but Barney Jonkman is going to stomp all over you."

Jerry, of course, had continued to demand at every appearance why Jonkman would not face him in debate. "What's he afraid of?"

Jonkman refused to debate him and thus let Jerry enjoy the role of underdog while many voters began to think Jonkman really was afraid of Jerry. Jerry later said, "Just being there in Congress, just hearing what is said in debate and in the cloakrooms, just knowing firsthand about legislation, gives the incumbent a great advantage. In a personal debate the incumbent is bound to seem knowledgeable about the job, and he can point out where the challenger doesn't have real knowledge."

In later years Jerry made it an axiom that he would debate any challenger to his reelection and he did so repeatedly and successfully.

So Jonkman's disdain or fear—it didn't matter which it really was—left Jerry with only one problem: He wasn't Dutch. Later events proved it was no problem at all, but Jerry didn't take any chances.

He roamed the sidewalks of the city, attended every meeting whose door was open to him, and coursed the farm lanes of western Kent County and of largely rural Ottawa County. He was sure he would get support among the Dutch if he could just meet enough of them.

"Hello, there. I'm Jerry Ford, running for Congress. Can I talk with you a minute?"

"Too busy pitchin' hay," the farmer replied, and Jerry had another inspiration.

"Mind if I help?"

"Fork right there, young man. Know which end to hold onto?"

Jerry shucked his coat and tie, rolled up his sleeves and commenced pitching hay. Soon he was talking about the election and the farmer was listening. It was a technique he used more than once, and, as he told his brother Tom, "It was one way to sandwich in some exercise." In later years, when Tom ran for the state legislature, he said more than once he encountered farmers who told him, "I remember the name;

your older brother pitched hay with me once when he ran for Congress."

The ethnic problem wasn't quite so easy, or so thought Jerry and campaign manager Jack Stiles. Jerry's looks could pass for Dutch but the name Ford simply wasn't Dutch and that's all there was to it. Later Tom said he himself had heard a *domker* (Dutch community leader) tell Stiles, "I like dot young man. If he vas Dutch, I vote by him."

"Oh, he's part Dutch," Stiles replied quickly.

"Ja? Den I vote by him," promised the elder.

But as it turned out the majority of Dutch voters didn't cast a straight ethnic ballot. In the primary Jerry defeated Jonkman 23,632 to 14,341, with 62.2 percent of the total vote, and he carried the largely Dutch Ottawa County by about 500 votes. In the general election he won with 74,191 votes, or 60.5 percent, over Democratic opponent Fred Barr's 46,972. He was not to receive less than that victory percentage until 1972, when he defeated Mrs. Jean McKee 104,045 to 65,775, or 60.3 percent.

The first victory is always the sweetest. And it was probably the cheapest. Tom, who was campaign treasurer, recalls taking in "about $4,000 cash." He added, "The volunteer help Jerry had was worth many times that. We had lots of it and lots of women. Our father always said that in politics a woman was worth three or four men because she'd work like a tiger if she believed in the cause."

He said even in that first campaign Jerry insisted a record be kept of contributors, by name and amount. Many contributions were "a five or ten dollar bill handed him on the street, and Jerry always made a record of the name."

In the primary Jerry had something else going for

him that has not been spelled out often or in detail in later political history. He had the active support of many liberal Democrats and of important labor leaders. No less a leader supported him, for example, than Leonard Woodcock, then a regional director of the Congress of Industrial Organizations (CIO), parent to the United Auto Workers International Union of which Woodcock later became president.

When Jerry won, there was a kind of nonpartisan celebration at Jack Stiles' country home at the northeastern edge of Grand Rapids. A supporter had bet fifty dollars that Jerry would carry Ottawa County and in the flush of victory donated the money toward the purchase of a formal wedding gown for Elizabeth (everyone called her Betty) Bloomer. Betty attended the party as Jerry's fiancée, happy that now they could be married.

Jerry Ford and Betty Bloomer had not been childhood sweethearts. It wasn't in the cards. He was five years older and already at the University of Michigan when she was a high school freshman. In those days that was a gulf seldom crossed, but they knew each other because Betty, squired by younger beaux, attended dances after football games at the University of Michigan. Then, after he had returned from the war and she from her dance studies in New York, they saw each other at parties and at dances. Attorney Kleiner recalls that she was very popular, "beautiful, lively and good company." And, after two years of studying dance under Martha Graham in New York, she was possessed of a certain glamor many Grand Rapids girls would not have had.

Their first real date was in the autumn of 1947, not many weeks after her divorce decree. She recalls that Jerry telephoned one evening to ask her out. She replied she had to work that night on a script for a style show the following day at Herpolsheimer's department store, where she was fashion coordinator.

"It was my livelihood," she noted, "but Jerry persisted. He asked if a short break from my work wouldn't be a good thing. So I said yes, and we went around the corner to a place and sat in a booth and talked awhile. How do we get around the fact it was a bar? Oh, well. And I don't know about Jerry, but that first date was it as far as I was concerned. Yes, he called me again soon, and there were many more dates that weren't so informal. We went steady just about one year before we were married."

Earlier accounts have recorded that Jerry proposed in May of 1948 but said that the wedding couldn't be until autumn because of "something that is coming up soon—I can't tell you about it yet."

It came in a few weeks when he filed as a candidate for Congress.

Kleiner said later he wasn't so sure about having helped Jerry get elected, but his donation for the wedding dress had been a great investment.

Now everything was go and the two were married October 15, 1948 in Grace Episcopal Church. A few at the wedding, including his horrified mother, noted that Jerry was wearing one brown and one black shoe. Even Jerry Ford could be a nervous and accident-prone bridegroom, especially since the November general election was not far off.

Jerry Ford's fiancée had actually been Elizabeth Bloomer Warren. She had been married six years to William C. Warren of Grand Rapids and had divorced him September 22, 1947, eight months before her engagement to Jerry in May of 1948. No previous account of the Jerry Ford, Jr., family mentions this fact, but the names on the wedding license and the divorce records of the Grand Rapids Superior Court attest it was so. The petiton was filed some weeks before divorce was granted, and it was suppressed. It alleged the usual "extreme mental cruelty and complete incompatibility" then necessary under Michigan law. The petition boiled down to the fact Warren was a traveling salesman and away from home much of the time. He had recently left home, in fact; the marriage had ceased to be a marriage. There were no children, there was little property beyond the furnishings of their rented apartment, which went to Elizabeth. The divorce was uncontested and the final decree was granted to her by Superior Judge Thaddeus B. Taylor on motion of Elizabeth's attorney.

Recently, Warren would say only that the separation and divorce were amicable. "We still have many mutual friends," he noted. After the divorce Warren went to Washington, where he married the daughter of a Mexican diplomat from Puerto Vallarta. He moved to Chicago and then San Francisco, where in 1974 he was an agent for furniture manufacturers and divided his time between San Francisco and Puerto Vallarta.

When the more than 430 FBI field agents staged their massive investigation of Jerry at the behest of Congress, many old friends and acquaintances of Jerry were interviewed. Warren was not. "Now I know what an un-person is," Warren told a Grand Rapids friend.

It was not a disgrace to be divorced in the Grand Rapids of that era. But on the other hand it was most emphatically not a political asset. Jerry didn't advertise his mother's divorce from his real father, or Betty's divorce. It was prudent politics in those days. The Dutch particularly frowned on divorce. Even up to contemporary times their moral precepts and church orientation have been so strong that in a devout Dutch Reformed church congregation, persons caught in adultery who did not want to be cast out had to stand before the congregation and confess their sin in explicit detail. Those who have heard such a ritual term it very traumatic, and not just for the sinners. The heritage of Calvin lived much longer in Grand Rapids than it did in such cities as Amsterdam.

10 The Early Years

Jerry Ford went to Washington to stay.

He took an empty briefcase; he had no pet bill or bold legislative program and no illusions about changing the world in one term. Mere survival in office would be accomplishment enough the first few years.

He took Betty, who found a cozy furnished apartment and proceeded to establish a homelife. And he took a smart office manager, a Grand Rapids man, of course, but one with special qualifications for his role. John Milanowski, then thirty-two and recently graduated from the Catholic University law school in Washington, had been admitted to the bar just weeks before Ford's election in November and was casting about for a place to begin practice. He was of Polish descent, short, dark-haired; like Ford he was political and ambitious. He agreed to run Jerry's office and be his alter ego for a few years.

Ford was assigned Jonkman's former office, room 321 in the old House office building. It was a rat's nest stacked high with every Agriculture Department report, every yearbook and manual given free to Congressmen. Stacks reached halfway to the ceiling; there was no filing system worthy of the name. The Saturday before Congress convened in 1949 Ford and Milanowski donned old clothes and went to clean house.

A Capitol guard stopped them and Milanowski had to explain, "This tall guy is Congressman Ford and I'm his assistant." It took most of the day to get the office clean enough for the new secretaries, Mildred Leonard and Adeline Brewer, both of Grand Rapids.

Life was more casual in the Capitol then. A young Congressman named John F. Kennedy, whose office was just down the hall, came often to chat with Milanowski. Both were bachelors. While still in school, Milanowski had invited Kennedy to speak to the Catholic University law club. He recalled that Kennedy regarded ordinary floor sessions of the House as "boring." Ford, however, learned to stay in his seat. In his first term he and Milanowski saw that being Speaker of the House was the best job in town, outside the White House ("second most powerful in government," Milanowski termed it) and one path to it ran through the House Appropriations Committee, where all budget bills must start.

"We talked about how nice it would be for Jerry to be Speaker someday," Milanowski recalled. "That's where all the patronage was, the power."

Jerry went on appropriations after serving his maiden term and then, Milanowski recalled, got a lucky break. George Mahon, Armed Forces Subcommittee chairman and a Texas Democrat, had a problem. The Army Corps of Engineers budget request called for study, analysis and a report on recommended action. Mahon asked if Ford and his assistant, being lawyers, could help. Ford agreed and the subcommittee liked the resulting report. Soon Ford came to be regarded as knowledgeable in defense-budget writing. He also served on the foreign aid and Central Intelligence Agency subcommittees of appropriations. He became the House expert on defense-spending budgets. Many of the 435 House members don't even read, much less understand, such bulky portions of the federal budget. Result: Ford was welcomed as a Very Important Person at any U.S. military installation in the world and in many capitals of undeveloped nations. He became something of a globe-trotter on Military Air Transport Service. And with the advent of the Republican administration of President Dwight D. Eisenhower and a Republican House in 1953, Ford became important in many circles while only a third-term Congressman.

He did not neglect the practice of politics. When in the last years of the Truman administration there was a scandal in the Federal Housing Administration, Ford and Nixon "screamed like eagles about it," in Milanowski's words.

Nor did they neglect the folks back home. They heeded the advice of Senator Frank Barrett of Wyoming to "be a clearinghouse for your constituents—help them with their troubles." As a member of appropriations, Ford's name was known throughout the maze of federal bureaucracy and in most departments or agencies he had a friend who could provide quick answers to questions or problems.

Callie Goebel, who served on the Civil Defense Advisory Council under three Presidents thanks to Ford, described it very simply in later years: "Many people never realized it, but in Washington Jerry Ford could open any door to help you, and he would."

Ford aided not just friends or wives of hometown mayors but anybody he thought deserved help. In his first years it came to the attention of the committee dealing with the armed forces that a young soldier somewhere in the boondocks was being disciplined because he had had the temerity to contact a Congressman about a personal problem. Ford had

Milanowski check the Selective Service Act, and they learned there was nothing in it giving servicemen the privilege any private citizen had—writing his Congressman. Clearly there ought to be a law. Staff aids of the Committee on Armed Forces, including Bryce Harlow, went to work drafting one, and it was passed with bipartisan support. It wasn't Ford's bill, but he gave it an enthusiastic vote.

One thing Ford did not do, even when he had power and opportunity for it, was grab big gobbets from the federal pork barrel for his own district. In 1973 a new federal office building opened in Grand Rapids, but even Democrats acknowledged it was time for a modern structure to replace what everyone in town called "the old post office." It was the biggest federal spending that could be attributed directly to Ford in twenty-five years. He had supported some antipoverty projects in his district, such as the popular Headstart project to ready children for school, but by no means all such programs. Naturally he argued that in Grand Rapids the poverty money was better handled than in the big cities.

Southern Congressmen who won military bases for their districts must have wondered how Ford got reelected. Ford's own view was, "Point one: You should practice what you preach. Point two: It isn't healthy for a community to depend on a federal payroll for prosperity."

Milanowski said frankly, "Jerry and I both were conservatives when it came to the taxpayers' money." Ford's starting salary was $12,500. Milanowski asked and got $300 a month.

Local Democrats and labor leaders felt Ford began as a liberal and quickly turned conservative. Milanowski's view was, "Jerry always was conservative, and he isn't going to change now." (Ford once speculated in an artless moment that now that he was Vice President and had a national constituency instead of a small and conservative congressional-district base, he might become "more liberal." The Atlantic City speech soon refuted that.)

In 1952 Ford had to make a decision. Arthur Summerfield, then the Michigan GOP powerhouse and chief fund raiser, asked him to run for U.S. Senate. The death of Senator Vandenberg had come with Democrat "Soapy" Williams in the governor's chair. Williams appointed the Washington correspondent of the Detroit *News*, Blair Moody, to fill out Vandenberg's term. Michigan Republicans wanted a champion to get the Vandenberg seat back where they felt it belonged. Summerfield, a Flint auto dealer, was to become GOP national chairman and Postmaster General. His advice carried weight.

Milanowski counseled Ford not to switch chambers of Congress. He pointed out Ford was rising in seniority, was likely to become top-ranking Republican on appropriations and from there would have an excellent shot at the speakership when the time was ripe. Besides, Milanowski noted, it costs a lot more money to run statewide for the Senate than it does to run in two counties. The bird in the hand. Ford diagnosed it the same way and decided against a senatorial bid.

This caused woe back home in Michigan. John B. Martin wanted to run for the Senate. Summerfield had a grudge against Martin and determined that Martin simply was not going to get the nomination. Ford endorsed Martin publicly. Martin ran in the GOP primary against Charles E. Potter, a Cheboygan welfare official with war wounds and two lucite canes that lighted up. Summerfield turned on the money spigot for Potter, who beat Martin and then Moody

Ford as a child with pet Boston Terrier.

Ford's mother, Dorothy, at age nineteen.

Young Jerry after a successful fishing expedition with a
chum.

The Ford boys gathered with their grandmother.
Jerry at right.

Ford posing for official grade-school photograph in Grand Rapids, Michigan.

Jerry, with "Ivy" Williamson, holding Most Valuable Player Trophy awarded him by the University of Michigan in 1934.

Ford's favorite hobby during vacation from Yale—sailing on Lake Michigan in 1938.

Marriage of Gerald Ford and Elizabeth Bloomer, October 15, 1948, at Grace Episcopal Church in Grand Rapids, Michigan.

Ford during service with U.S.
Navy in World War II.

Ford at work in his office, 1973.

The Fords as snow architects. Left to right: John, Betty, Jerry, Sue, Mike, and Steve.

in the general election. But Potter was a weak incumbent and in 1958 Democrat Phil Hart took the seat from him and kept it.

By 1955 Milanowski itched to go back home to Grand Rapids and do some lawyering. He wasn't getting rich in Washington and he would always be a subordinate in the shadow of his elected tiger if he stayed. The opportunity came when a Grand Haven, Michigan, schoolteacher, Frank Meyer, joined Ford's staff under a Ford Foundation study grant. Meyer worked into the staff well and after a year Milanowski begged to go home. "Frank is a bit straitlaced but he will be loyal to you," Milanowski said. Ford released his aide to a greater destiny and later was influential when in 1969 President Nixon appointed Milanowski district attorney for Western Michigan. Until his death in 1972 Meyer was Ford's trusted assistant. His death was one reason Ford could not explain all the details of his campaign contributions, because Meyer had handled them. Just as Milanowski had made out Ford's income-tax returns and "even baby-sat for the Fords." Ford needed good staff help, then and later.

Every Ford staff member quickly learned to give every possible consideration to constituents' problems and to visitors in Washington from the home district. Eventually a Polaroid camera was installed on a tripod as a permanent office fixture: The visitor would be photographed with Ford if he were in the office, or sitting at Ford's desk if he were out. If there were good reason to open a political door the petitioner couldn't find or didn't know about, it was opened to him. Better yet, Jerry Ford would make the inquiry and mail the answer back. It usually went out within forty-eight hours.

A job? Jerry Ford was almost Jacksonian in his belief that any honest, capable person deserved a crack at a federal job if there were an opening. One had but to ask.

In late 1951 I applied for a post abroad in what was then the U.S. Information Service. As an afterthought I asked Congressman Ford if he would give a letter of character reference.

Would he? Such a letter! It greeted the official in charge of the hiring as an old acquaintance, mentioned a mutual acquaintance Jerry had met while passing through Old Delhi on an inspection tour in the Orient. The letter reminded him that Ford had consistently supported the Voice of America budget and then in a closing paragraph said I was applying for a job and any consideration would be appreciated. I got the job.

In three months I was en route to Saigon.

A year later the ubiquitous Congressman Ford flew into Saigon on a tour of U.S. military installations in the Far East, which included consultations with embassies and inspections of foreign-aid field programs. The French armies were supposed to be winning the Vietnam war at that time. Later during a chat back home in Grand Rapids, after Dien Bien Phu, Ford conceded the French may have "dragged their feet" in Vietnam, but that was as critical as he would get. He was a real hawk on Vietnam, from the first.

After his three-day visit in Saigon he flew back to Korea, where he saw the first prisoner-of-war exchange at Pånmunjŏm, and met General William Westmoreland. He came to like "Westy" enormously and their friendship grew. Westmoreland visited Grand Rapids to make a Memorial Day speech at Ford's request. After he became Vice President, Ford said in answer to a question that there was a time when he, like Westmoreland, thought the Vietnam war could have been won militarily, but it was so long past there was no point regretting it.

From 1954 to 1965, when President Johnson committed fighting units to combat in Vietnam, was a long time. During that span of uneasy peace Ford was to rise from congressional importance to real power and to disagree publicly with Johnson—not over entering the Vietnam conflict but over fighting a limited war.

But jousting with a Democratic President was a long way down the road; it could not have been foreseen in 1954. The election of Eisenhower in 1952 opened a new and, he hoped, a Republican, era. With any luck that Republican era might last beyond Eisenhower's expected two terms. Given peace and stable times, the future was bright for younger Republicans. Funny thing, however, at times Ford seemed to have too many futures dangling before him.

For instance, did billionaire Howard Hughes try to buy Jerry Ford a Senate seat? Ford himself was never sure but thought it possible.

In the mid-1950's Ford had two more opportunities to run for higher office, with offers to subsidize his campaign expenses. He turned down both and was always glad he had. Neither offer, Ford said, was ever "generally known." The first was under most peculiar circumstances.

A delegation of very conservative Republicans came to him in 1954, Ford said, and offered "unlimited campaign funds" if he would run against incumbent Republican U.S. Senator Homer Ferguson of Michigan in the primary. This was not as outlandish as it might sound. It was true, Ford noted, that in the first Eisenhower administration Ferguson had become one of the top Republicans on the Senate Appropriations Committee and a strong supporter of the President's budgets. But Ferguson was not conservative enough for the Republican Old Guard. In loyalty to the administration he had cast a key vote against the "Bricker Amendment"—a measure Eisenhower interpreted as limiting his ability to conduct foreign affairs.

But, Ford said, he heard two "stories" explaining why the right-wing Republicans asked him to run in the primary. Ferguson's vote on the Bricker Amendment was the first. The other story, Ford said, was this: "In 1945 Homer had been a member of the Truman investigating committee, and he had been quite critical of Howard Hughes [over war contracts] along with Senator Ralph O. Brewster of Maine and I guess some others. And Howard Hughes never forgave either Brewster or Ferguson. The story was that the people who came to see me allegedly had been urged to do so by some of Howard Hughes' friends. That was the second story. But since I wasn't interested, it didn't make any difference. I told them, number one, I was loyal to Homer, and number two, I was starting to move up in the House and I thought that the best place for me to make it was in the House, leadership or otherwise. So I turned them down. But those were the stories. I don't know which was right."

The next offer, Ford said, came in 1956. President John A. Hannah of Michigan State University approached Ford to offer his services in raising campaign funds if Ford would run for Michigan Governor against G. Mennen "Soapy" Williams. Williams had swamped a weak Republican candidate in 1954 and was becoming a legend in his own time. (He ultimately served a record six two-year terms and retired undefeated in 1960.) But Ford didn't want to retreat to a purely Michigan environment, and he was not convinced he could build a statewide constituency in time to beat the formidable "Soapy."

Ford was doubly wise. The men who ran against Williams are now all but forgotten except among Republican old-timers.

11 The Middle Years

Sometime after 1955 Jerry Ford left Grand Rapids, mentally, and became a Washingtonian with a specific personal ambition. But it was not apparent. Because it was so gradual, Ford himself may not have realized the metamorphosis.

Looking back, 1955 to 1965 were the bluebird years for Jerry and Betty Ford in Washington. The family rounded out. Steve and Susan were born, joining Mike and John; their home in Alexandria was purchased and a swimming pool built. Relative to what had gone before and what would happen starting in 1965, it was a decade of stability, of happiness, of hard work and hard play. Congressional leaders still believed in a summer recess, in lots of time for campaigning in election years, a good winter holiday. The nation rested at peace, queasy as the peace was. Prices were stable and one did not need a high income to live comfortably.

Jerry perfected his people-pleasing machine. His staff developed a system that was near-science: Not a sparrow should fall in the fifth district without Ford's office hearing of it and trying to do something to help. If there were Dutch immigrants with friends in Grand Rapids (and there were) who needed help entering the country or applying for citizenship, Jerry Ford's office in Grand Rapids or in Washington would move fast to ease the way. If there were Latvian doctors, refugees from Russian hegemony, who were seeking a new home (and there were), Ford stood equally ready to help. The publicity value was not neglected. Newsmen back home in Grand Rapids had a story: "Every Dutch immigrant to Grand Rapids since Jerry Ford went to Congress just happens to have been an underground resistance hero during World War II; and every Latvian who wants to come to Grand Rapids was the leading physician in Riga before the Russians took over." It was an exaggeration, of course, but Jerry's staff never neglected a sympathy angle in their ombudsmanship.

They would have laughed at that word. In those days it was called "serving the people of our district," and they did it willingly, instinctively, rapidly. If you walked into one of Ford's offices and asked for a drink of water, they would try to turn on a fire hose. And if, later on, you cared to make a political campaign contribution, what was wrong with that? As Ford's prestige rose in Congress and his relations with the White House grew, so did his power to help.

After 1952 Ford's prospects had brightened. Election of Republican President Eisenhower enhanced the prestige of the Republican representative—on the important military affairs subcommittee of House Appropriations. The election especially helped Ford, who was building a reputation as a hard worker, a faithful Republican, a team player, a comer. It was not until 1963 that he would challenge any incumbent Republican leader.

In his first year in Congress, his first vote on a significant issue was to reduce the House Rules Committee's power over legislation. Truman had won election in 1948 by lambasting the "do-nothing Eightieth Congress." So reformers of the Eighty-first Congress looked to a chief roadblock, the Rules Committee, which could kill any legislation it disliked simply by not reporting out the bill, but sitting on it. A House majority adopted a change, known as the twenty-one-day rule. Under it committee chairmen could bring bills to the House floor if the Rules Committee refused to act on them within twenty-one days. Ford was among those Republicans who joined the Democrats to vote for the bill; one of the Republican nay votes was that of Representative Richard M. Nixon.

Sixteen years later, in his first roll-call vote after having become GOP Minority Leader, Ford would vote against reviving the old twenty-one-day rule.

But during the 1950's Ford voted against a move to kill Truman's "Point Four" program of aid to under-developed nations. He opposed a bill sponsored by Democratic Senator Robert Kerr of Oklahoma to stop federal regulation of natural-gas prices. In 1951 he supported continuation of livestock-slaughter quotas—a device to control meat prices and combat black-marketeering. In 1956 he supported the first civil rights bill to pass Congress since the post-Civil War Reconstruction days. In 1957 he voted against Southern amendments aimed at crippling the pioneer civil rights act, which established a Civil Rights Commission and an assistant attorney general for civil rights with authority to seek court injunctions to protect individual rights.

The Americans for Democratic Action published annual ratings of Congressmen's liberalism or conservatism, depending on votes in such areas as civil rights, congressional reform and consumer-protective legislation. In his first year, Ford cast what the ADA considered to be a liberal vote on 13 percent of the bills studied. This rating went up to 30 to 40 percent in the early 1950's, 60 percent in 1955, 57 percent in 1956, and culminated with 67 percent in 1966. Ford was issue oriented. He liked to explain it this way: He was "an internationalist in foreign affairs, a moderate in domestic affairs and a conservative in fiscal matters."

He was healthy; he had one of the best attendance records in the House; he believed a Congressman was there to vote, not to duck out on controversy; he cast thousands of recorded votes during his quarter-century in the House.

With that mass of statistics it was possible to make him out a nice guy, a moderate, a middle-of-the-roader, or a Genghis Khan, depending on how you played the statistical record.

Ford remained consistent while the mood of the times veered liberal and some politicians moved with that mood. His opposition to school busing to achieve integration was almost instinctive; he didn't believe in the concept. Michigan Democrats almost tore their party in two at the state level as they first endorsed busing and then ran from it like the plague when they learned how voters really felt. Ford, graduate of what was at the time an integrated and a good school system, reacted the same way his constituents did.

Jerry was the product of a conservative town. Brother Tom said that in 1930, when avowed Socialists and Communists were painting slogans on walls of public buildings in Grand Rapids, Jerry led an after-dark foray of South High School athletes to halt it. Tom said they caught some young leftists at work and dumped their paint over their heads. In that same era a group of Grand Rapids leaders lay in wait for an announced march of political leftists on city hall, and met the demonstrators with tarpots and brushes in hand. They marched the protestors to the city limits, whacked on some tar and warned, "Don't come back." The same civic leaders were among the first to organize soup kitchens and flophouses for the hungry unemployed.

From 1955 to 1965 Jerry also sat on the small (five-member) subcommittee on Central Intelligence Agency appropriations. There he learned some things one could not talk about at the family dinner table. As he noted years later, he knew about the U-2 photographic spy plane before it was ever built. The U-2 was a good idea except that eventually the United States got caught using it—and over Russia at that. President Eisenhower said he didn't know it was going on—over Russia. Later Eisenhower had to back away from that flat statement and admit he did have prior knowledge. The effect on world opinion was devastating.

In Japan Eisenhower's press secretary, James C. Hagerty, was negotiating with government officials on an impending state visit by Ike. Left-wing students and young political radicals snake-danced in front of the American embassy, set fires to American cars with diplomatic license plates and howled against the perfidious American president. They were encouraged by some Japanese leaders, including a member of the Japanese Diet who was pictured in newsreels and television film dancing atop one of the American autos and urging on the student rioters.

After the smoke had blown away in Tokyo and Eisenhower's visit had been canceled, to his great disappointment, somebody got an idea. Why not go to Japan at next election time—after all, members of the Japanese version of Congress have to run for election, too—and try to defeat the so-and-so who capered on that car and encouraged the kids to whoop it up against Ike?

And it was done with the help of the CIA dirty-tricks division. The idea came from a former Michigan Congressman who also executed his own idea. He was an astute politician and he later told intimates, "It was easier to do than it would be to defeat an incumbent here; and as you might expect, all it took was money."

Ford ought to have known about it, considering the circumstances. If he did know, he probably enjoyed the fact the CIA could win one victory, however insignificant.

In the 1960's Ford traveled even more, and he began to become a familiar face on the Republican Party Lincoln Day dinner and fund-raising circuit. He estimated that the number of such engagements rose to hundreds a year. His day often went like this: Rise early, go to the Capitol at 7:00 A.M. or so and do office work, receive visitors, confer with Republican associates, attend committee hearings. Noon: Attend convening of the House, stay awake during debate or confer with cronies in the hall on upcoming major business. At 2:30 or 3:00 P.M., grab a briefcase with work papers and a speech text, a plastic garment bag, with a change of suit and shirt, and rush to Washington National Airport to fly to the speaking engagement. Make speech. Fly home, arrive at 1:00 A.M. Take a relaxing swim in the pool. Sleep five or six hours, then repeat. By the time he had become one of the "great leaders" in Congress, he had the routine down pat.

His first modest taste of formal leadership came in 1963. His game plan aimed right at the Speaker's rostrum, but he found it expedient to move up through the chairs, starting with one of the lowest.

Young Republicans and those like Jerry who were outside the Old Guard power structure had been disappointed many times. Eisenhower had been elected twice but could not sweep a Republican Congress into office with him. So there were no committee chairmanships to pass around. What power Republican House members did have was concentrated in a few hands, most of them Old Guard. And the election of John F. Kennedy in 1960 by the thinnest of margins presaged more dry years. The off-year congressional election results in 1962 were none too satisfactory. Had the Republican party blown it again? The moderates and progressives wondered. As the new Congress convened in 1963, Republicans began to mutter among themselves about revolt against their leadership.

Ford talked with his career consultants, Bob Griffin of Michigan and Charlie Goodell of New York. A revolt plan was cooked up, but private polling among the GOP membership indicated it would fail. So they supported Charlie Halleck to continue in his post of Minority Leader and ran Jerry against Charles Hoeven of Iowa, the Republican Conference (caucus) chairman. Hoeven was then sixty-seven; Ford was forty-nine. Ford won. He began talking up the idea of "positive Republican programs" to offer in bill form, instead of just opposing every Democratic administration program, a revolutionary thought to some of the mossbacks in the Republican hierarchy. And always in Jerry's mind was that magic number—218—the number of votes it took to elect a speaker.

12 The Warren Commission
Interlude

Jerry Ford led a charmed life, close to the center of history. He was in the heat of the fighting against the Japanese. He visited Indochina just months before the French forces were defeated at Dien Bien Phu. He stood at Pånmunjŏm, Korea, and saw the first American prisoners of war return after the armistice. He was to become the first Vice President nominated by a President and confirmed by Congress. In 1964, between winning his first party leadership post and becoming House Minority Leader, came an interlude of unusual service and a saddening experience.

In November of 1963 President John F. Kennedy was assassinated by Lee Harvey Oswald. The following month Lyndon Johnson, as the new President, appointed the Warren Commission of seven, including Ford, to investigate and report definitively on how the assassination was accomplished. After the slain President was buried, the nation had begun arguing three assassination theories:

One, that Oswald was a lone maniac, incredibly lucky and a marksman with a $12.50 rifle; two, that Oswald was merely a none-too-bright executioner in a Communist plot that might have started in Russia or Cuba; three, that there had been a homegrown American conspiracy to bring about Kennedy's death, and some forces in Washington, possibly CIA agents, were mysteriously involved.

President Johnson, who would have to seek election in his own right in 1964, wanted the doubts and the whispers quieted before the election. His appointees, led by Chief Justice Earl Warren, were predictably dubbed "a blue-ribbon commission." Certainly its seven members had impeccable reputations: Warren, Ford, Senators Richard B. Russell and John Sherman Cooper, Representative Hale Boggs, Allen Dulles, former director of the CIA, and veteran diplomat John J. McCloy.

Ford was an active member of the commission from the start. The investigation obviously called for a sizeable staff, including professional investigators. Commission members would want on that staff someone they could trust to ensure that the inquiry wasn't taken over and managed by an interested group. Ford picked his first campaign manager and longtime friend, John R. Stiles of Grand Rapids.

President Johnson made all facilities of the federal government available, but this was a mixed blessing. Stiles said afterward the competitive feeling between the FBI and the Secret Service was a big problem, one of several, in setting up a modus operandi. The total job took six months. Ford had to strive night and day to keep up normal duties in Congress and stay abreast of the investigation's spadework.

In September of 1964 the seven commission members were satisfied that they had reached, unanimously, the only logical conclusion. That they were ready to report. But for reasons of his own President Johnson delayed publication of the report for days.

On September 20 I telephoned Ford and asked the question on the minds of millions: Would it be wrong to think the commission had determined that one man alone had planned and executed the assassination? No, said Jerry, it would be "an accurate assumption" by a newsman. Furthermore, he, Ford, didn't know why the President was holding up the release. It was ready.

Six days later Johnson allowed it to become public —on a Saturday. The White House press section was well aware that a Saturday-morning release would give double-barreled coverage: first in Saturday's news reports by all media and then in lengthy excerpts and analytical pieces in the thick Sunday newspapers. Maximum exposure. The thick volumes were passed out Saturday morning and were snapped up by every major publication and news service in the noncommunist world. It became a best seller for a short period.

Ford became an author as a result of the Warren Commission service. It was Stiles' idea; writing was his first love, especially historical writing. He wrote much of the book, but Ford worked hard at it, too. Ford later said he found writing "hard work." The book, titled *Portrait of the Assassin*, did not sell well. People who buy books, it seemed, believed the Warren Commission report. And if Oswald had not been part of a diabolic conspiracy, the story was less interesting.

When the book was published in 1965, so much was happening there were plenty of excuses to put Dallas and Oswald in the attic of the mind. It was obvious many Americans wanted to; just thinking about it hurt. Perhaps the book was premature by a generation.

13   He Rises to Power

The inaugural of Democratic President Lyndon Johnson in January, 1965, was a four-day Texas-size bash. It had elements of Mardi Gras, New Year's Eve, homecoming football game, barbecue, with the black ties and mink capes falling a little askew as the booze flowed and happy predictions were shouted over the din of many parties. Millionaire ranchers and black bellhops fraternized, assuring each other the nation was fortunate to have their man, good ole country boy Lyndon, running it.

Johnson had won the biggest landslide victory since 1936, a mandate to keep the peace and prosperity flowing, plus, of course, the equal opportunity for all races and help for the poor that Johnson had promised in his campaign.

Many Republicans simply joined the partying. They had feared Barry Goldwater would lead them to defeat; he led them to debacle and Republicans who survived the landslide considered themselves fortunate. One survivor was Governor Romney of Michigan, who had won with a respectable 342,914 votes over those cast for Democrat Neil Staebler.

Jerry Ford was waiting in the wings. He didn't waste any more time partying than he had to. He had been talking with his close associates since November election day. He had come to town the first of January with a plan for revolt.

The Republican Representatives who survived the

Democratic landslide faced a bleak four years with fewer troops and less power. They had lost thirty-eight seats. It might have been worse, yes. But they were tired of telling each other that election after election. When the devil was it going to get better? The minority-party mentality might be all right for Minority Leader Charlie Halleck, but not for a soldier in the ranks who had hope of a committee chairmanship, a large office and staff, power and prestige.

Halleck, sixty-three years old, was a crony of "Judge" Smith of Virginia, Democratic chairman of the powerful House Rules Committee. Halleck shared the conservative political philosophy of Southern Democrats as well as their appreciation of good whiskey. He never worried much about the plaints or ambitions of the "youngsters" in the House. He hadn't gotten the message when Ford replaced Hoeven as conference chairman, not even when Hoeven himself noted that the 1963 revolt was really against the top leadership. "I was picked as the lamb for the slaughter," Hoeven said at that time. "This should serve as notice to Les Arends [party whip] and Charlie Halleck that something is brewing."

Brewing was a prophetic word because the rebellious Republicans (by no means were they all young) had no unanimity the day after the 1964 election. Goodell had begun planning in late 1964 to push Mel Laird for minority leadership. Ford not only wanted to go for the top job himself but to replace all the existing GOP leaders with his own supporters. The kettle was aboil and time was short.

Right after the election Representative Thomas B. Curtis of Missouri had written a letter to all House Republicans suggesting the idea that they get together for a conference. This letter was seized upon by Ford and company as a trigger for their own move, and they moved fast. Conference chairman Ford had the right to call such a gathering but only if there was a demand for one. Michigan's Bob Griffin called six revolt-minded Republicans to a secret meeting in his office and got agreement to contact, in the name of all seven, the other Republicans and urge that they write Ford, as chairman, and request the conference. When the number of planned requests reached a mere thirty, Ford sounded the call to meeting on December 6.

On the surface it was bland as baby formula. Halleck appeared to take over, as if nothing were boiling under the kettle lids. But the evening of December 6, after the formal conference, Goodell gave a cocktail party in his office for sixteen red-hots who were not about to give up. The group included such conservatives as Ford's good friend and contemporary Elford A. Cederberg of Bay City, Michigan, as well as the young Turks. It was a cross-section of the House GOP. The talk ran late into the night. Laird was discussed first, but a nose count showed too many moderate and liberal Republicans were angry with Laird, who, as platform chairman of the 1964 national convention, had tailored the GOP platform to Goldwater's hardnose taste.

So it was decided Ford would be the strongest candidate.

Griffin put together a team of approximately thirty determined rebels: The young would recruit the young; the older and more conservative would work within their peer group. They kept at it almost thirty days—until midnight, January 3, eve of the showdown leadership caucus.

"It will be close, but you will win," Griffin and Goodell reported to Ford after a final nose count.

114

When the ballots were counted, Ford had seventy-three votes, Halleck sixty-seven. The honor of nominating Ford had gone to his friend, Cederberg.

Ford did not get everything: Arends remained as whip. And in a contest between two of his supporters for conference chairmanship, Laird and Peter Frelinghuysen of New Jersey, the more conservative Laird had won. Ford said he wanted someone "wholeheartedly behind the new legislative strategy." When Laird won that post, Ford asked Frelinghuysen to seek the post of party whip, which he did, but unsuccessfully. By that time the Old Guard had become the underdogs and evoked enough of a sympathy vote that Arends survived the rebellion.

All this for titles that sound meaningless to the ordinary voter?

Yes, indeed. Not meaningless at all, if one stops to consider the nature of Congress. Political purist John V. Lindsay, who was a Congressman before becoming Mayor of New York, once observed despairingly: "It is a little difficult to say with pride that ours is a government of laws and not of men when power and prestige in Congress are not won, as they should be, through diligent, intelligent achievement, but are rather awarded to the winners of the continuing race against time." A penetrating thought and beautifully phrased. And devastatingly accurate.

But Ford and his rebels had proven the exception to Lindsay's dictum. It had happened before in history, although not often. Old "Uncle Joe" Cannon, doughtiest Speaker of them all, had wielded absolute power many years and lost it in a rebellion. Halleck himself had led a successful revolt against Joe Martin.

Ford had come up through the ranks and was, with Senate Minority Leader Everett M. Dirksen of Illinois, top-ranking Republican in government—a potential Speaker, if his party could ever get out of the habit of losing at the polls.

To that end Ford went to work immediately. The concept of thinking out, articulating and offering "positive Republican alternative programs" to the big-spending Democratic programs was prepared for action. It was a first in GOP congressional history. Ford also replaced the untelegenic Halleck on the Republicans' television show. It was now *The Ev and Jerry Show*, and to the surprise of political liberals and drama critics it became popular. Dirksen was a consummate ham, with a good sense of timing, completely unpredictable, and possessed of a resonant voice that flowed as rich and sweet as farm-table sorghum. Ford played it square, an ideal straight man for the old maestro of the Senate GOP.

Then commenced a period that for Jerry Ford was cakes and ale, politically speaking. He became a national figure to the corporate community, even though he was unknown to the mass of voters. He became a sought-after speaker, the kind who rates an honorarium plus travel expenses, if not a company airplane to ferry him from Washington. He never milked that honorarium opportunity for very much income, but at least travel was no drain on his own purse. Ford would later estimate that in 1966—which was to be a happy year for Republicans—he made 200 speaking trips. One of the few who didn't regard it as a vintage year was Betty Ford, who stayed at home with four active children to raise.

Another piece of cake on Ford's desk was that the President was a Democrat. The administration programs would be liberal and expensive. They would be anathema to many Southern Democratic mossbacks, to state's-righters and conservatives. To get his major programs through the House, Johnson would have to ask Republican help. If a program failed, it would be the Democrats' fault because they were in numerical majority. If it succeeded, Republicans could also take credit for the good in it.

Johnson didn't wait long to launch his war on poverty, just as he did not wait long to launch his war in Vietnam. The year 1965 was when history's tempo quickened faster than at any time since Pearl Harbor day, 1941.

Johnson outlined his antipoverty program in a general way at the University of Michigan commencement, May, 1965. Governor Romney sat beside him on the football field where Ford had played. The big Texan, who sized up the afternoon sun and took off his suit coat before donning an academic robe (they had made him an honorary doctor of law) was about to launch one of the biggest giveaway programs for big cities in history. Romney chided him in the helicopter that bore them away from the field and urged the President to consider the plight of the states, too. (Romney came to hate the poverty program's wastefulness and seemingly to hate Detroit Mayor Jerome P. Cavanagh, whose offer of his city as test laboratory for the poverty program was accepted. Almost $100 million poured into Detroit in the period between 1966 and 1972, before another President could wind down the Office of Economic Opportunity and close many of the money funnels.)

When the program's dollar signs appeared in printed bills before Congress, Ev and Jerry recoiled in horror, too. But the needs of the core cities were so great, the "Republican alternatives" such pale gruel in comparison to the Johnson plan, that the war on poverty was an unstoppable idea. Besides, a new phenomenon appeared—the graduated federal income tax in a time of high employment and ever-rising personal income was producing so many billions that even Johnson had a hard time spending them all. The money was there. And Ford saw some good in the OEO catalog. Grand Rapids got its share in Headstart for kindergartners, which was as popular in suburbia as anywhere.

Even though Ford now had power enough to do it, he did not pile the budget with pork for his fifth district, not even when the Vietnam war could have offered an excuse to open a military installation or subsidized industry. In 1971 federal spending in the fifth district was $663 per capita, $1,019 nationally. Ford declared then and afterward it wasn't wise to base an economy on a military payroll or a war. He preferred a diversified civilian-economy base. But such ideas received little public airing. There was a war on.

Johnson started with a few regiments of military advisers and left office with more than half a million men in Vietnam. Ford the hawk went him one better and urged the President to unleash the Air Force to bomb North Vietnam much harder. Why fight a war with one arm tied down? he demanded. He was for naval blockade of North Vietnam. He was entirely free to criticize the tactics of the Democratic President and did.

"Jerry Ford is a nice guy, but he played too much football with his helmet off," Johnson told newsmen one day in exasperation at the GOP opposition in the House. Johnson had a gift for cutting remarks, and the House could be exasperating.

As Republican leader, Ford found it to his advantage to work with Southern Democrats on many occasions. He didn't hesitate to collaborate with them when it helped Republicanism—but not on Halleck's crony-style drinking-buddy basis. Ford kept it on a basis that was as ethical as possible. Moreover, he liked and respected Speaker John McCormack. The line of communication went from Johnson to McCormack to Ford, and back up the same way.

In 1965 the voting-rights act passed with Republican help. Cederberg declared afterward it could not have happened without Republicans like Jerry supporting it, because "there weren't enough Democrats willing to vote for it." The act was a landmark in black history and paved the way for election of blacks in Southern areas where trying to register to vote had historically been an invitation to loss of job, a beating or lynching.

In 1967 Ford voted against a $1.75 billion appropriation for the OEO, to eliminate the model-cities program, and against federal money for rat control; he voted for state control of poverty programs in 1969.

By 1971 Ford voted 87 percent of the time with the preferences of the Conservative Coalition grouping and against many measures favored by labor unions, Americans for Democratic Action, environmentalists, "Nader's raiders" (especially in the field of auto-emission controls), frequently even against legislation favored by farm groups. (Ford deplored the wheat-subsidy program that led to "growing for storage." The fifth district was not a big wheat producer.)

Ford knew well the duties of a Minority Leader: to be chief strategist, organizer, and allocator of committee assignments to members of his party; to keep vigil over the rights, prerogatives and traditional privileges of the minority; to know what is in legislation coming before the chamber; to be father confessor to rookies and younger members.

He campaigned for the job on a simple platform: "No man's light will be hidden under a bushel; every Republican will have a voice in decision-making and a chance to make a name for himself."

His methodology was just as simple: to listen rather than lecture, to be sympathetic to the views of other people, however they might differ from his, to be tolerant, and to avoid a loyalty showdown over each and every roll-call vote on each bill. He was sympathetic to the principles of others; he had often voted his own convictions, although he knew it could be a luxury as one moved up through the chairs to the top.

By the end of 1971 he had voted 3,436 times on the procedural movement or passage or failure of legislation. In December that year he took five pages of the Congressional Record to explain his votes during the year as he had done at the close of each annual session. He commented, as usual, he wanted to be able to provide "my interested constituents with a simple compilation of my voting and attendance record." It was part of the people-pleasing mystique: Give 'em a full report.

How enjoyable were the election results of 1966 compared to those of 1964. Ford was still half a light-year away from the speakership, but the numbers tell the tale: In 1964 the Republicans had only 140 seats in the House or 32 percent of the 435 total. As a result of the 1966 election their strength went up to 187 seats or 42 percent. (In the Senate Republican strength went from 32 percent to 36. One of the newcomers was Bob Griffin of Michigan.)

In Michigan Romney was credited with carrying Griffin to victory, and the maverick Governor won with a landslide of 568,448 votes over Democrat Zolton Ferency, a firebrand who frightened half the members of his own party. Republicans also recaptured the Michigan legislature, elected a state supreme court justice and some university board members. It was a genuine landslide. Nationally Republican leaders declared Romney the "front runner" for the 1968 GOP presidential nomination. A good technique, as it turned out, to set an aspirant up for a shooting gallery.

Ford's power grew. He and Dirksen gave their own GOP State of the Union message for the third consecutive year and made it clear that Republicans in Congress intended to have a strong voice in Vietnam war policy and further shaping (and funding) of Johnson's Great Society.

In his book *The Minority Party in Congress*, a penetrating study of congressional politics, Charles O. Jones pointed out there was something new in Republican history—a minority party not only offering its own positive legislative program but getting significant parts of it passed into law. Jones, the Maurice Falk professor of politics at the University of Pittsburgh, wrote: "House Republicans were notably successful in building majorities for their own proposals in 1967—a remarkable achievement for a minority party. On occasion it appeared the Republicans were the majority and the Democrats the minority."

Professor Jones cited such examples as their role in shaping the elementary- and secondary-education bill, which gave state departments of education greater responsibility. Another example of Republican strength was their "principal victory" in shaping the Law Enforcement and Criminal Justice Assistance bill (originally proposed by Johnson as the Safe Streets and Crime Control Act). On a key issue of giving block grants to states rather than categorical grants to local governments, the Republicans won their version on a vote of 256–147—a coalition of 172 Republicans, 16 Northern Democrats and 68 Southern Democrats. Such coalitions are seldom accidental; Ford and his lieutenants had done their job well, behind the scenes.

It was the very essence of congressional politics, and Professor Jones observed: "It may well be that [ten years later] the experiment of adopting aggressive policy-making strategies will have been merely . . . one more experiment. It is clear, however, that the House minority party in 1966 and 1967 attempted to take greater advantage of its strategic position than ever before in this century. This is not to say the minority-party members have not been innovative or clever or positive in the past, but the minority party itself never had organized to the extent that it did in these two sessions to influence the process of majority building."

Organization and preparation were fifty percent of the battle, and Ford knew it. Having the votes was the rest of it. And the first could lead to the second. That's how he got to be Minority Leader—and survived as Minority Leader.

Ford was no orator, and he let others do much of the speechifying on the floor of the House. But he could give a strong speech when he wanted to, and in mid-1967 he decided the time was ripe. Johnson had asked Congress for a ten percent surcharge on individual income tax—not enough to cope with the inflation that was beginning to creep through the nation's economy—but just enough to escalate the war another notch. The casualty rate was rising. The American generals wanted more warm bodies.

On the floor of the House Ford delivered what was for him a jeremiad, not against the Vietnam war it-

122

self but "after much reflection to express grave misgivings about the way the war is going."

He noted that with the tax message asking the surcharge the President had announced his decision to authorize at least another 45,000 troops to be sent to Vietnam in that fiscal year. Ford said in part: "This will swell the total to five hundred twenty-five thousand Americans. Vietnam is a major war and has become an American war. At the end of 1963, when President Johnson succeeded to the presidency, the United States had sixteen thousand men in Vietnam; only one hundred nine had been killed in action and about five hundred wounded.

"By grim coincidence, the Pentagon released the latest casualty figures the same day we received the President's tax increase message. The toll [as of July 29] stands at eighty-seven thousand—twelve thousand dead and seventy-five thousand wounded in round figures.

"I blame nobody but the Communist enemy for these sad statistics. I have supported the President and our country from the outset and to this hour. I have heard myself branded a hawk and worse for counseling firmness against Communist aggression and using America's awesome arsenal of conventional arms to compel a swift and sure peace. But I am troubled. Recent surveys show that more than half of our people are not satisfied with the way the war in Vietnam is being conducted.

"Mr. Speaker, why are we talking about money when we should be talking about men? The essential element in President Johnson's tax message is not higher revenues but human lives—not whether every American shall live better but whether hundreds and thousands are going to live at all . . . [That is] a question crying for political courage of the highest

123

order—to admit past policies have been woefully wrong. I believe everyone in this House would vote any level of taxes and the American people would willingly pay them if convinced it would bring the Vietnam war to an end. But as I do not believe the grave challenges we face at home can be countered simply by pouring out more and more money, neither do I believe the great challenge in Southeast Asia can be met by pouring in more and more blood.

"The President said the inconveniences of his tax plan are small when measured against a Marine on patrol in a sweltering jungle. And who can question such a comparison?

"But the question we may ask—and the one I must ask—is this: Why and how long must Americans, now nearly half a million—wait ten thousand miles from home to meet and match Asian enemies man to man, body for body?

"Why are we pulling our best punches in Vietnam? Is there no end, no other answer except more men, more men, more men?

"General Eisenhower recently stated pointedly that a 'war of gradualism' cannot be won. What is especially dishonest is secretly to forbid effective strategic action and publicly portray it as an honest try. Then, when expected results are not forthcoming, to belittle the effort and its backers. This is worse than dishonest—for meanwhile brave men have died in vain.

"This is not a Democratic war nor a Republican war. . . . My party has in fact stated its support of the war more explicitly and muted its public criticism and dissent more successfully than the President's party. Republican policy on Vietnam generally has been based on a very precise and wholly nonpartisan statement which I helped to draft and to which

I consistently contributed for the past twenty months. It was issued December 13, 1965, by the National Republican Coordinating Committee."

Ford noted that it contained a warning against "growing eager" for involvement in a land war in Asia . . . that the first objective should be to impose a "Kennedy-type" sea quarantine on North Vietnam, that America should use to maximum its conventional air and sea power.

Ford said he came to some "tragic and troubling conclusions": The American policies and purposes in Vietnam had failed; stalemate and deadly attrition were the only achievements; Republican policy suggestions were being ignored completely; only one-quarter of the known oil-storage targets had been hit by American air strikes . . . only three of every ten significant military targets had ever been struck by U.S. airpower.

Ford listed several categories of targets—transportation, industrial plants, ammunition dumps, troop centers—and gave precise statistics on how few had been touched. He repeated the phrase "Why are we pulling our punch?" many times.

"Maybe the President has some scheme for getting the country out of the war as invisibly as he got it into the war," Ford suggested from a columnist's attack on the Vietnam policy.

"I believe the test of will and courage is not the people's but the President's. I believe ending the war must have the highest of national priorities, now.

"I do not want to wait until the 1968 elections in the United States to bring this war to an end. If bringing peace and bringing half a million men home alive would ensure President Johnson's reelection by a landslide, I would gladly pay that price. I don't think the President has made a convincing case

125

for a tax increase. Let us debate that another day. Even less has the Commander in Chief made a convincing case for sending forty-five thousand more troops to continue a ground war in Vietnam. It is my earnest plea that he will reconsider."

There it was in one package: the frontal political attack, the basic disagreement on how to fight a war, the appeal to stop a slaughter by winning the war, the Republican distaste for a tax increase. Ford had talked with former President Eisenhower and former Air Force Secretary Stuart Symington, as well as Republican party leaders and high-ranking generals in the Pentagon who chafed at the limits on their strategy imposed by Johnson and his advisers.

The Vietnam war policy was delineated as the overriding national issue, the issue to decide the 1968 presidential election. It had been given to Ford to sound the call to Republicans to get going on the issue. And the speech hit the most sensitive nerve in the Democratic party.

The 1966 elections showed the first of the antiwar sentiment among the general public. Johnson even then was losing popularity. After the election, at a winter conference of Governors in West Virginia, the Democratic Governors held a midnight caucus. Many reporters wondered what kept them so late. In fact they were discussing Vietnam and Johnson and their party's future. Their conclusion: If the war news continued bad into 1968, the Democratic party was going to take a bath and President Johnson couldn't "get reelected dogcatcher."

Attorney Richard Nixon was working hard on the Republican dinner circuit. His Vietnam policy was "an honorable peace, followed by American withdrawal." There was no articulation of details, no explanation of how to do it. First, he would say in the

New Hampshire presidential primary campaign, "What's wrong with winning?" Romney, stuck with a seventeen-point Vietnam policy that confused everybody, would withdraw from the race in February, 1968, long before election day.

Ford got under Johnson's skin and it was no wonder. And no accident. The years 1965 to 1967 were Ford's heyday of punch-out politics. As in football, somebody won, somebody lost.

The years 1968 to 1970 were more difficult. Republican Nixon was elected President. The end of the war was nowhere in sight. Creeping inflation became running inflation. The federal budget soared in dollar total. The cost of welfare programs became staggering during the greatest prosperity the nation had ever known.

Minority Leader Ford had to carry the mail for a President of his own party. The speakership was still as far away as ever. The House Republicans had gained only five seats in the 1968 elections. When would they ever find the key to a majority in Congress? Perhaps when Nixon ran for reelection in 1972, when the war had ended. Ford wished it mightily and worked to that end. He put the best possible face on things. He began predicting an honorable end to the war. In 1970 in Michigan during a talk with an old friend, former publisher Louis Weil of the old Grand Rapids *Herald*, Ford declared optimistically that the war was winding down, that the President's policies were working, and expressed a thought that American troops might be getting out of Vietnam that Christmas.

By that time Ford's fifth district was no longer Kent and Ottawa Counties, it was Kent and its eastern neighbor, Ionia. Ottawa had been on the west. Ionia was mostly rural, with not many voters of

Dutch origin. At first Ford was unhappy because he would be leaving the service of many good friends and acquaintances in Ottawa County, and Ionia was new to his experience. It worked out all right because Ionia remained politically conservative while Ottawa was acquiring more Democratic residents in a westward drift of population.

But it was not of his choosing. The Michigan legislature held the power of drawing new congressional districts and had gone at it in clumsy fashion.

The state had eleven Republican Representatives, eight Democrats. The Democratic party hoped to change that ration in a state ordinarily thought of as Democratic. But with the legislature oh-so-narrowly controlled by the Republicans, it would be hard to carve new districts favoring the Democratic party. Unless the Democrats could strike a deal. And they almost did.

Lieutenant-Governor at the time was a Democrat, T. John Lesinski, a lawyer from the tough Polish enclave of Hamtramck, surrounded by Detroit. A superb parliamentarian and a master at political deals, Lesinski talked eleven Republican state Senators into agreement on a plan that would give Democrats a better edge in southeastern Michigan and the Detroit metropolitan area.

Lesinski's deal was partly executed before Romney and other Republican leaders woke up. (Romney had been traveling more than usual, for one thing.)

Ford, Cederberg and other Republican Congressmen were furious. They burned the telephone lines back to Michigan with profane demands to know what was going on and what had happened to a supposedly resurgent Republican party, especially the glamorous Romney administration with all its class and charisma.

Romney moved decisively once he woke up. At a dramatic meeting of Republicans he called the truant Republican state Senators "political quislings," and other bad names. The situation was straightened out in a few weeks, and the ensuing congressional-district plan was one everybody could live with. Even through the 1972 elections the Michigan delegation remained eleven to eight Republican in the U.S. House.

It was an example, however, of the troubles a long-time Congressman can have back home. The voter might assume a Republican administration at state level would work hand-in-glove with its Republican delegation in Congress, or Democrats with Democrats. Not always so. As every Congressman knows, the home folk want to know, "What have you done for me lately, and what can you do tomorrow?"

Governor Romney particularly gave Ford fits. Ford once told me after a number of years' living with Romney in the Republican party, "George Romney is the most stubborn man I ever met in politics!"

During the latter part of Romney's tenure as Secretary of Housing and Urban Development, a Michigan lobbyist for a school group had occasion to learn and make use of the edgy relationship between the two strong-willed men. His employers wanted a new facility, to be administered by Grand Rapids Junior College, for the education of registered nurses. The three major Grand Rapids hospitals were starting to phase out their own training programs.

The lobbyist related this account: "I and some others went to Washington with our plan; we needed federal matching money. We decided to try HUD because it had some money and there was legal basis for the plan, but it was something new to HUD's experience, it would be a first. Romney said, 'No way.'

Then we went to Jerry Ford's office to talk about our plan. I told the need, which Jerry knew existed. I told about the plan, which could work. We just needed about one hundred eighty thousand dollars at the start from HUD. The community was doing its share of the financing. Ford listened. But when I said we had been to Romney's office and he turned us down, Ford really got interested. He said, 'Just a minute.' He picked up the phone and called somebody in the White House. We got our money—from HUD. The nurse-training facility is in use today."

Ford found the next Republican Governor after Romney, William G. Milliken, much less abrasive. Milliken had an entirely different character, no ambitions for the presidency and much respect for Senator Griffin, who came from his hometown, Traverse City. But, politics isn't always easy.

Ford's brother Tom had become a state legislator in 1966. He represented the district that included East Grand Rapids and the former Ford family home. It had some suburbs and farm country in it, too, and was conservative.

Milliken became Governor in 1969 and soon showed the same liberal tendencies Romney had, and then some. Milliken insisted the city of Detroit and its troubled school system be given financial help. He saw eye-to-eye with Democratic leaders on a number of social programs.

State Representative Tom Ford opposed many of them. He was an effective speaker, with a gift for terseness. And he lost his reelection bid in 1972. He then asked the office of Governor Milliken for help getting a job on the state payroll—having cashed out of the family paint business when he moved to Lansing as a legislator.

Milliken's staff said bologna to Tom, and Milliken

agreed to remain adamant. Tom let Jerry know about it, and along about that time a routine request came through William McLaughlin, Michigan GOP chairman, asking Ford's help in getting a federal job for a deserving state Republican. Congressman Ford sent word back to Milliken through McLaughlin "that cooperation works both ways, and I was disappointed they hadn't done anything for Tom."

The friend Milliken wanted to help was State Representative Michael A. Dively, Republican from Traverse City—a hometown buddy. Dively was an able young lawyer; he had supported Milliken's legislative programs. He wanted to move into a bigger political scene, and the job he had in mind was director of ACTION—a Nixon device to phase out the overseas Peace Corps and Stateside Vista program, by merging them into a volunteer-service organization.

But Milliken was adamant against hiring Tom; Ford remained obdurate on recommending Milliken's friend; Dively stayed in the Michigan legislature.

When it was revealed publicly that President Nixon had bombed Cambodia and planned to invade it long before he told Congress, Milliken was among the public figures who condemned the secrecy of the move. This stance evoked Ford's wrath. Ford was preparing a press release expressing his displeasure in strong terms. He privately expressed anger that Milliken would set himself up as a "military expert." A visitor from Michigan, a friend of both Ford and Milliken, talked Ford out of the public blast at Milliken.

There were troubles like that, not big ones, of course. But they happened.

The year 1972 convinced Jerry Ford that his future lay in retirement. If, in the biggest landslide in American political history, the Republicans couldn't carry the House, they never would. He planned to run "one more time" in 1974, serve out that last term and then bow off the scene. That was his plan until October 12, 1973.

14 Diversions and Excursions

Over the years a lot of people had looked for a corrupt stain in campaign contributions made to Ford, or through him to others. Often the search was made by newsmen routinely checking out leading politicians, sometimes by persons with other motives. In more than twenty-five years no one had ever made an allegation stick; no one had come up with evidence of fraud, lawbreaking or personal enrichment. Some Congressmen were venal enough or stupid enough to deposit contributions to personal checking accounts and later claim carelessness. Not Ford.

With Ford it was the $2,000 or $200 out in sight, and the list of such contributions grew long in his later congressional years. He was not, as others suspected, a bag man or a "funnel" for secret millions. He was an effective fund raiser for the Republican Congressional Campaign fund and for himself. Over the years the legitimate funds he handled added up to hundreds of thousands, and those who knew him were convinced every penny of it was legal.

One of the allegations that must have irked Ford came not from a newsman or a Democrat but from John Childers, legislative assistant to Republican Senator Charles H. Percy of Illinois. Childers told Percy that Dale Schaufelberger, a director of the Agricultural and Dairy Education Political Trust, told him that "two people associated with the Illinois dairy industry had visited Washington to bring money to Congressman Ford for distribution to other Congressmen in connection with the 1973 farm bill."

Childers said Percy told him to write a memorandum to the Senate Rules Committee investigating Ford prior to confirmation as Vice President, and he did.

The various parties involved were interviewed by Jack W. Germond, then chief of the Gannett news bureau in Washington, and reporter Peter Behr. Schaufelberger, an Illinois dairyman, told them he never made the accusation and would so testify under oath. Gary E. Hanman of Missouri, chairman of the ADEPT group and purportedly one of the contact men, denied any such donation, although he had "talked with Ford on occasion" about farm legislation. Childers said he had the definite impression that a donation was tied to the eighty-five percent price parity support the dairymen sought, but added he considered what he heard "strictly hearsay."

In the newspaper article by Germond and Behr it was stated that undisclosed "other sources" had it that Ford told Schaufelberger he needed $15,000 to distribute among political friends, presumably for their campaign debts.

This was not confirmed by Childers; it was denied by Schaufelberger and Ford. Ford stated, "The milk producers' counsel, Bob Collier [a Washington lawyer], came to see me after the election [of 1972] and said his clients wanted to help Republican members who had campaign debts. I checked with Jack Calkins [executive director of the Republican Congressional Campaign Committee] as to who had obligations, and I gave Collier a list of six or seven names. He turned it over to his clients. I then promptly forgot about it.

"A month or two later several milk producers came

into my office and wanted to give the money to me. I told them, 'No, if you want to make a contribution to these members, you will have to give the contribution directly to them.' Apparently they did, and I assume the contributions were reported. I have no other knowledge as to the facts of this matter."

The Gannett news story noted there was "no evidence to indicate Ford did anything in behalf of the dairy industry. He was not among the members of Congress who sponsored the special bill for milk price supports as 85 percent of parity, the milk producers' goal at the time."

The Senate Rules Committee went into this and many other details of Ford's handling of contributions over the years. It found nothing at which to cavil. Nor any violation of law.

Ford himself had received many contributions during 1972: They totaled $94,000, of which only about $10,000 came from his home state.

The largest single sum came from a fund-raising dinner in the familiar Capitol Hill Club: $38,216. The money was turned over to the Ford for Congress Committee. Ford had another ad hoc committee working for him, the Friends of Jerry Ford Committee, and in Washington there was a group that called itself the Committee to Reelect Jerry Ford, which was formed to stage the $38,216 dinner. It then disbanded and did not file a report, nor was it required to under prevailing law. (Each year as Governor of Michigan, Milliken was beneficiary of a similar dinner, which yielded as much as $130,000 in a night.)

Ford's total 1972 receipts also included $16,925 from political-action committees of various organizations and $3,625 from various Republican committees.

Ford in turn passed out part of his receipts with a

generous hand: His old friend Bob Griffin, up for re-election, got $3,000; another friend, Al Cederberg, got $750, as did Representative James Harvey of Saginaw; Representatives Charles E. Chamberlain of East Lansing and Marvin L. Esch of Ann Arbor, $1,000 each; Reps. Garry E. Brown of Schoolcraft and Robert J. Huber of Troy, $500 each. In all Ford passed out $16,650 to other Republican Congressmen seeking reelection, including friends in Iowa, Nebraska, Utah, Ohio, Minnesota, Mississippi, Colorado, North Carolina, Indiana and California. More thousands were parceled out to local Republican candidates in Michigan and to some county Republican committee campaign funds.

The list of individual contributors to Ford in 1972 contains some monied and important names: Joseph M. Segel, president of the Franklin Mint, $2,546; Grand Rapids businessman Ralph Hauenstein, $1,000; New York attorney David S. Smith, $1,000; Richard Scaife, a Mellon heir, of Pittsburgh, $2,500; New York businessman John M. Shaheen, $3,000; Edward J. Frey, president of the Union Bank in Grand Rapids, $2,000.

There were many contributions of $500, $300, $200, many of $100 each. Most contributions were from business and professional people, from New York to California. Bloomfield Hills, Detroit's posh executive bedroom community, was an address that appeared frequently on the list. There were many smaller contributions, but the bulk of the Ford money came from the $100-and-up categories.

To the taxpayer all this history might sound as venal as an airline's contribution of $100,000 to the Committee to Reelect the President. There's no arguing morality, but the fact is that Ford's receipts were legal, the airlines' contributions were not. The practice of taking contributions from the business people was old as the hills; the law that requires detailed reporting took effect in 1972 and brought the practice to public attention. Anytime the electorate cared to do something about it, there were and always would be ways. And it's only fair to note that the giants of organized labor don't have to report the thousands of man-hours they can pour into the campaign of a favored candidate. Many Democratic candidates would rather have this kind of contribution than the thousands of dollars the business individual can give a Republican.

The millions that were available to the Nixon campaign in 1972 from milk producers, oil interests, and corporations, added up to a big scandal. Against that background Jerry Ford looked clean and was clean.

Jean McKee, the Grand Rapids lawyer who was the last Democrat to run against Ford for Congress, said, "You'd have to catch Jerry Ford smuggling heroin into the country to make people in Grand Rapids think he was dishonest."

For instance Ford had been appointed a director of The Old Kent Bank, the largest in Grand Rapids. The emolument involved was $1,000 a year, and Ford considered it more of an honor than anything else. He borrowed $3,000 elsewhere to buy stock in the bank and meet the stock-ownership requirement of a director. He was genuinely surprised, and said so, when the Grand Rapids *Press* criticized him editorially and pointed out how it might become a conflict of interest when banking legislation moved through Congress. Ford mulled this over for a time, then resigned from the directorship. It probably had not occurred to him that some people might think he could be influenced in Congress by a bank directorship back home. In his own case he had forgotten the phrase "Not just honor, but the punctilio of honor."

However Jerry Ford could make a mistake, and when he did, it was apt to be a beauty. His experiences with G. Gordon Liddy and Robert N. Winter-Berger were dramatic examples. In the first instance Ford innocently did Republican friends a favor by helping Liddy get a federal job; in the second he was duped when he should have heard alarm bells. The results were disastrous, and it was a minor miracle Ford did not become the laughingstock of Washington. But others were duped, too, and Winter-Berger made the mistake of writing a book.

Liddy was a former FBI agent who thought a man couldn't be too zealous in his patriotism. The "former" was by will of the FBI, not Liddy. He became an assistant prosecutor of Dutchess County, New York—the kind with a police radio in his car and a collection of pistols at home. For some "missions" he called for pistol number one and for others it would be pistol number three, or maybe number four, depending on the nature of his excursion.

Not content with that, Liddy ran against Hamilton Fish, Jr., candidate for Republican congressional nomination in the Poughkeepsie area. He lost the primary to Fish and then went to work for the Citizens for Nixon-Agnew drive in Dutchess County. Ford flew there to speak on behalf of Fish and the GOP ticket at a political rally in the general election campaign. He recalled Liddy as one of the majordomos in charge of the rally.

Ford himself gave this account: "After I spoke, Dutchess County Republican leaders including Ham Fish came to me and asked if I didn't know of some job in Washington that might appeal to Liddy. I didn't know him at all, but he seemed energetic and they seemed anxious to help him, so I said I would see what I could do.

"It turned out they were anxious to have Liddy move on, out, go some place else. I remember their telling me he was a political puzzle to them, because they didn't know whom he might run against next time." (But nobody told Ford about the gun collection and sirens in the night.)

After the 1968 election and advent of the Nixon administration, Ford recalled, he was given a biographical résumé by Liddy and a handful of endorsement letters from Dutchess County leaders including Fish and GOP Chairman George Reid. Liddy told Ford he would prefer a job in the enforcement division of the Treasury Department or a job in the Justice Department.

The White House staff had thousands of job openings, and an office especially set up to match job seekers with jobs available. Ford sent Liddy's dossier to that office and also called Eugene T. Rossides, then head of Treasury's anticrime division. The time was April, 1969. Rossides gave Liddy a job.

"I didn't pay any more attention to Liddy after that," Ford said when the Watergate scandal broke out in 1973. "He was just one of the many persons I tried to help get jobs at the time."

The next time Liddy came to Ford's attention was during Treasury's much-publicized "Operation Intercept," which President Nixon had thought so well of —at first. The "operation" consisted of massive methodical searches of all vehicles entering the United States from Mexican border points. The traffic jams, especially when the technique was invoked at the beginning or close of a weekend, were massive. There was never any warning, and many thousands of honest Mexican and American tourists and commuters

139

experienced delays of twelve hours and longer. The agents who had to do the systematic searches of everything from a retiree's camper to a hippie's mini-van were as unhappy as the customers. The result was much marijuana confiscated, at first, and mass frustration. The practice was abandoned after strong protests by the Mexican government.

Liddy, naturally, was a key honcho in Operation Intercept. In 1971 he left Treasury.

"The next I heard about Liddy," Ford related, "was when it was announced he had been named general counsel of the Committee for the Reelection of the President in 1972. . . . I wondered about it because by then I'd begun to pick up things, you know, that made me wonder about him."

Ford didn't know it in 1971, but Liddy had moved to the White House and become a member of the "plumbers squad." Liddy was one of the masterminds of the burglary of Democratic Headquarters at Watergate. After the resulting trial before Judge John Sirica he was sentenced to six to twenty years for the break-in as well as a contempt sentence for refusing to testify before a federal grand jury. One thing that can be said for Liddy: He didn't rat on his employers. It was part of his twisted code of patriotism *über alles*.

Liddy was a tragicomic figure and his downfall predictable. His involvement with Ford was slight, but it was a sad comment on job-giving in federal government. The more Liddy goofed his roles, the higher he went. Right to the White House plumbers unit where, one believable story has it, fellow conspirators found it advisable to warn Liddy that assassination was not a way to solve the problem of Jack Anderson, the syndicated, muckraking columnist who was so critical of the Nixon administration.

The Winter-Berger story is equally bizarre and involved Ford up to his eyebrows. Robert Winter-Berger was a New York public-relations man and jack-of-all-affairs who turned to lobbying in Washington when he acquired clients with political problems. In 1964 he was introduced to Democratic House Speaker John W. McCormack of Massachusetts by Nathan Voloshen, an influence peddler of the first rank who operated from the Speaker's office and, Winter-Berger claimed, actually paid $450 a month rent for the privilege. Winter-Berger said Voloshen introduced him to McCormack as a specialist who could help get the aging Speaker a "national image" and build him up as a potential vice-presidential nominee. This homemade boomlet was launched and then died in a matter of weeks, but Winter-Berger stayed on for years, commuting to Washington almost daily by plane or train. In 1966, Winter-Berger said, he decided to establish rapport with Republican leaders in the House of Representatives and paid $1,000 for an introduction to Ford.

Winter-Berger reasoned that an introduction from someone Ford knew would win his confidence quicker than a direct approach. He knew Alice Weston, a former actress, then with a public-relations firm, whose family was rooted in west Michigan and has close association with the Ford family of Grand Rapids. Miss Weston wrote her brother, Peter S. Boter of Holland, Michigan, and he in turn wrote a letter of introduction for Winter-Berger, describing him as a client of his sister who had some matters he wished to discuss with Ford.

Winter-Berger said Miss Weston then went to Washington with him to meet Ford, who in 1966 was into his second year as Minority Leader in the House. Contact was established.

Winter-Berger said he "decided to level" with Ford, told him he was a lobbyist who had been "working out of McCormack's office two years" and now wanted to work with Ford. He claimed he also said he was not interested in "carrying tales." He claimed Ford responded favorably and told him, "I think we can work together. . . . My only interest in money is raising money for the Republican party. I prefer not to see your wallet. When you think a contribution is legitimate, send me the check."

Winter-Berger funneled thousands to Jerry Ford and conceded later that Ford always insisted it be in the form of a check, made out to a campaign committee or most often to the Republican Congressional Boosters Club—a continuing slush fund to reelect GOP Representatives. He later said that Ford never put a penny of the money in his own pocket, although he accepted $500 for campaign fund-raising dinner tickets one time.

But Winter-Berger did have access to Ford's office and Ford's ear. He was well traveled and a cultured person in comparison to Ford. (He once said, "Ford came to Congress as an unabashed country bumpkin.") And he was a quick learner in any milieu. He was facile, articulate, a skilled public-relations man and publicity writer, a polished climber and cynical student of human frailty. He declared in his book that Speaker McCormack's first words after meeting him were, "The motto around here is 'nothing for nothing.'" He claimed Ford told him more than once, "Money is the name of the game here; without it you're dead."

They may have said just that or words to that effect. Ford never tried to kid anybody that money was not the lifeblood of politicking; he argued that as the reason good citizens should support good candidates.

But it also is true that Ford tried to help some of Winter-Berger's clients, and there is the point at which politicians flirt with the flame. A notable example was l'affaire Kellogg. Francis Kellogg of New York was president of International Mining Co. A man of means who liked big-game hunting, he wanted to be named an ambassador to an African nation and asked Winter-Berger how to go about it. Winter-Berger said the key was large donations of money to the Republican party, now that President Nixon had been elected. Winter-Berger said Kellogg gave $125,000 in all, including $30,000 to the Republican National Committee through Ford.

He said he had approached Ford and found him unenthusiastic about Kellogg until he mentioned the $30,000. Then Ford quickly became interested.

Ford later conceded he had helped Kellogg and noted that the would-be ambassador had to settle for a brief visit to Africa as a conference delegate and a middle-echelon political post in the State Department, not an ambassadorship.

In his book, *The Washington Pay-Off*, Winter-Berger gave Ford a most dubious compliment, that of all the politicians he had dealt with, he found Ford most willing to try to repay a favor.

Ford had parted company with Winter-Berger in 1969, long before the book was published in 1972. In a first-chapter footnote Winter-Berger made the unusual admission: ". . . throughout the manuscript I have relied on my memory, which is excellent, as well as on notes I had made, to register conversations of which I have firsthand knowledge. In many cases the conversations are verbatim as they occurred. Even when they are not, the sense and substance are strictly accurate." In other words a purported direct quote might just be paraphrase.

The book was full of quotes by high personages, including one Winter-Berger attributed to the late President Johnson, who, he claimed, came in anguish to Speaker McCormack's office to ask help in muzzling former Senate Secretary Bobby Baker, then under indictment, and including a declaration by President Nixon that "any friend of Jerry's is a friend of mine"—in a context of helping a lobbyist's candidate get a high-ranking federal post.

Many of the quotes and many of Winter-Berger's allegations were considered libelous, and some book dealers would not stock the volume. There were many denials by the persons he named, as well, and Winter-Berger had no tape recordings or documents to back what was in the book. He had a particularly bad time before the Senate Rules Committee, which held public hearings on Ford's nomination as Vice President. Asked how many times he saw Ford during the period between 1966 and 1969, he replied, "I could not be precise. . . . It was about eighty times."

That was one of the smallest details. Winter-Berger conceded that he had not even kept a diary in which to record the sometimes-lurid conversations and the dates on which they allegedly occurred; that his writings contradicted subsequent testimony that he had lent Ford $15,000 cash over the three and a half years of their acquaintance; and that he had no documentary evidence of such a loan; that he turned government witness against his sponsor, Voloshen, when the latter was indicted for illegal lobbying, "because it's survival of the fittest"—his choice was testify or be prosecuted. He described himself as an influence peddler and was, now, not very proud of what he had done.

Winter-Berger even gave two versions of why he had stopped seeing Ford. One, that in October of 1969, once he had become a witness against Voloshen, he cut off their association because it would have proved embarrassing to Ford. The other, that one day, Ford simply told his staff never to return a Winter-Berger telephone call or let him into the office. "I got the message," Winter-Berger said.

Even New York Congresswoman Bella Abzug, who said she would not vote for Ford's confirmation as Vice President, accused Winter-Berger of using Ford as a pawn. Several members of the Senate committee indicated they couldn't believe anything Winter-Berger said. The question of possible perjury was turned over to the Justice Department for investigation. There had been no report on that investigation by beginning of 1974. But by 1974 Winter-Berger had become small fry; the Justice Department was busy with much greater matters.

In his own testimony before the Senate and House committees Ford acknowledged the visits, the checks for GOP campaign funds, recommending Kellogg to the State Department for a job. He denied categorically the main thrust, that Winter-Berger had bought his friendship, his office and influence, and he denied that he had ever taken a penny from Winter-Berger for himself. And some of Winter-Berger's details—such as Christmas presents for Ford's staff: wallets with $100 bills in each—Ford and his staff declared to be outright lies. Ford's personal secretary told a friend that Winter-Berger gave her "a thing to put money in that might have cost five dollars, and it was empty."

After Ford was sworn in as Vice President he said in a private interview that Winter-Berger "always held himself out as being very knowledgeable, knowing what was going on in Washington, knowing important information."

Asked if he ever offered to peddle information about the Speaker's office, Ford replied: "Twice he began conversations to the effect that he knew so much about Voloshen and what was going on that if he told it, it would be very damaging to the Speaker's office. I stopped him each time and told Winter-Berger I wanted to hear no more along that line, that I had a high regard for John McCormack and good relations with him. I told him not to start that line of conversation again."

Asked how a Winter-Berger could happen to him in the first place—which was the question in the minds of ordinary voters—Ford would only say, "Some people are deceitful," and repeated, "some people are deceitful."

It was a closed chapter in Ford's mind. He just did not want to live it over again. It obviously hurt him.

There is no other explanation: He was naïve; he had been gulled. How could he accept political contributions from a Winter-Berger and not get smirched? Some money does stink—and always will. The best that can be said about the sordid affair is that it was part of Ford's political education, and high time.

Publication of Winter-Berger's book naturally created a storm back home in Grand Rapids. The Grand Rapids *Press* asked for statements from Winter-Berger and Ford and wanted to know what evidence there might be to corroborate the allegations. The Washington bureau of the Michigan newspaper syndicate, Booth Newspapers, called

Winter-Berger in New York. He said he had a bank-vault box full of documents. Booth reporter Robert Lewis flew to meet Winter-Berger, who took him to a bank to look at "letters and other documents." Lewis reported he was shown nothing that appeared to be evidence, just a collection of papers any lobbyist might have. He interviewed Winter-Berger at length. His notes showed that Winter-Berger said, "Jerry Ford never personally received a cent from me." Winter-Berger told him he gave wallets to three of Ford's employes at Christmas, 1967, but said nothing about $100 bills. Lewis reported this in the Booth Newspapers and gave an affidavit detailing the visit to the congressional committees holding hearings on Ford's nomination.

The disturbing fact was that until publication of his sensational book Winter-Berger was not known to many in Washington, certainly not to the press corps or to the majority of Congressmen. But he was known to some very important people, such as McCormack and Ford. One experienced Washington lobbyist declared, "Washington is crawling with Winter-Bergers. There are people here making sixty thousand dollars a year just because they can introduce a businessman or somebody with a problem to an official in the federal government who deals in the area of their interest or their problem. . . . And many times they would get the same hearing without the influence peddler. Sometimes not, of course."

Ford, possibly without realizing it at first, helped Winter-Berger build himself a certain sphere of influence that became marketable. The money from that market might have been legal by the time Ford got some in return, but it wasn't very clean. The fact that many other Congressmen had done the same thing was no reassurance to the American voter.

15 Impeachment

"What, then, is an impeachable offense? The only honest answer is that an impeachable offense is whatever a majority of the House of Representatives considers it to be at a given moment in history; conviction results from whatever offenses two-thirds of the other body considers to be sufficiently serious to require removal of the accused from office—there are few fixed principles among the handful of precedents."

Strong language, from Minority Leader Jerry Ford, April 15, 1970. Later he must have wished it could be expunged from the Congressional Record and forgotten. When asked to reconcile those words with his stated belief in 1973 that President Richard M. Nixon had done nothing that was impeachable, Ford explained he felt that there was a significant difference between reasons for impeaching a judge and for impeaching a President.

He declared to his fellow representatives in the House that, look here, we define the offense, and then the Senate tries and judges the matter in the context of our charges. There was precedent for this: Jurist Thomas Cooley in *The General Principles of Constitutional Law* had said in 1931 that impeachable offenses were "any such as in the opinion of the House are deserving of punishment." Senator Benjamin Butler had made the same claim about the impeachment of President Andrew Johnson.

Ford's 1970 definition was very blunt and very political, not partisan-political but political in the full sense of the word—historically accurate, but also an admission that the impeachment process could be open to excess and abuse.

Ford's target was a judge: Supreme Court Justice William O. Douglas, who had been on the court since his appointment in 1939 by President Franklin D. Roosevelt. A liberal judge who believed the American Constitution was a living and growing document, a dissenter against the doctrine of strict construction, Douglas was also an author, mountain climber and outdoor enthusiast. At an advanced age he had married a twenty-two-year-old law student. He was the darling of parlor liberals and the intellectual left; a dangerous radical, a swinger and a dirty old man to the political right.

And there he sat on the nation's highest court. The Democrat-controlled Senate had rejected President Nixon's nominees to that court: good Southern conservative judges, Clement F. Haynsworth, Jr., of South Carolina, rejected by the Senate on November 21, 1969; on April 8, the following year, the Senate had rejected G. Harrold Carswell. Not since 1930 had a President's Supreme Court nominee been rejected; the White House was furious, and so was Attorney General John Mitchell.

Ford's attack on Douglas was launched in a national atmosphere of hostility toward "liberal courts." Alabama Governor George C. Wallace expressed it in this ineffably demagogic way: "A man hits you over the head at night to take your wallet, the judge will set him free before you get out of the hospital, and they'll prosecute the policeman who arrested him."

The hostility was not confined to House Republicans for whom Ford spoke. There were Southern Democrats just as red-hot as any to strike back at liberalism by assaulting the Supreme Court's most publicized liberal. When Ford made his speech asking a special committee to investigate and report whether grounds existed to impeach Douglas, he had popular support on both sides of the House aisle.

It was, in the handling and execution, in the articulation, unworthy of Ford. At times he sounded like a farmboy at the carnival, demanding that sheriff's deputies raid the kootch dancers' tent. He actually carried with him, to show reporters, a magazine containing an article by Douglas juxtaposed to a photograph of a naked woman, which he termed pornographic. No Ford-watcher would ever believe he had rummaged through magazine displays seeking just such a weapon, much less that he had stumbled on it accidentally—a fact that was later confirmed.

No, Ford was also carrying the mail for the White House. The Justice Department, then headed by Mitchell, gleefully fed Ford what information it deemed best-suited to the assault, an assault that demeaned both Ford and Douglas. But Ford insisted it was his own idea, that there was no prompting from Nixon, Haldeman, Ehrlichman or Mitchell. And that may be, but there was implicit encouragement all through the Nixon administration and overt huzzahs from conservatives in both parties in Congress.

Ford later said, after becoming Vice President, "Impeachment would have been too harsh, and perhaps what I did was too strong." It is not clear whether he was trying to rewrite history or trying to reveal a motive not apparent at the time of his impeachment effort.

For that mild admission there would be no thanks from Douglas or from the outraged "Eastern liberal press," which had long ago ensconced Douglas in its ideological pantheon.

Ford's view of the episode, in retrospect, made himself a kind of Republican hero in a complicated situation. If his account is accurate, history might take less harsh a view of Ford's assault on a liberal justice's integrity. It was not a clear-cut horse opera situation, where the bad guys tried to ambush the good.

Ford declared in an interview in early 1974, he was actually trying to stave off impeachment proceedings against Douglas, and most particularly a move by ultraconservatives to introduce an impeachment resolution first and then study the merits later. "There were five in the House ready to go—as I recall, three Republicans and two Democrats. I thought impeachment would be too harsh, and looking back what I did was perhaps too strong," Ford said.

His basic motive?

"What I wanted to do," Ford explained, "was establish one standard, for sitting judges as well as presidential nominees—to establish that there should not be a double standard. The message wasn't just for Democrats, it was for liberals in both parties."

And send them a message he did. If the Senate had balked at Judge Haynsworth's financial investments as a built-in conflict of interest, and at Carswell's political ideology, then let the liberals consider the record of Justice Douglas.

Ford's bill of particulars contained a handful of main points:

One: Douglas had dissented in a 5–4 decision upholding a pornography conviction of *Eros* publisher Ralph Ginzburg in 1966.

Two: Douglas dissented in a decision giving Senator Barry Goldwater a libel judgment against

Ginzburg in 1969. That same year the magazine *Avant-Garde*, with which Ginzburg was associated, paid Douglas a $350 fee for an article. ("Gross impropriety", declared Ford.)

Three: A book by Douglas, *Points of Rebellion*, was inflammatory.

Four: The article opposite the nude picture, "Redress in Revolution," in *Evergreen Review*, was, well, if not a clear call to revolt, at least unworthy of a Supreme Court justice. Courts, in Ford's view of democracy, were meant to protect the system's institutions, not to preach "revolution."

Five (and here his argument was on more solid ground): Justice Douglas had received an annual retainer of $12,000 from the Albert Parvin Foundation, which, some said, received skim-off money from Las Vegas and was too friendly with Mafia figures. The Douglas association was well-documented. He was also a consultant to the Center for the Study of Democratic Institutions, which got Parvin Foundation money. (A month after Ford's opening attack Justice Douglas discontinued his association with the Parvin Foundation.)

Ford's demarche did not win its objective—a special committee to investigate. But he did get a special judiciary committee investigation. Ford said in retrospect that was what forestalled an actual move to impeach. He noted that a petition of impeachment, once filed, hung on the House calendar like a bomb with the longest of fuses. At any time during the legislative year any member of the House had the privilege of rising to move its adoption. The speaker, according to the rules, had to give the motion priority over any other business.

Ford, the legislative tactician, said that was one thing he did not want on the House calendar. Considering Ford's commitment and dedication to his job as Minority Leader, the petition per se would be enough trouble potential, regardless of one's judgment on Douglas.

The subcommittee to study impeachment reported the following December, just before adjournment of Congress, that it found no grounds for impeachment.

Bob Hartmann, Ford's administrative aide at the time, had an interesting perception of the whole affair. In 1974 he said that on the merits he felt Douglas was most vulnerable because of the Parvin Foundation retainer and least on the *Evergreen Review* article. The question was one of the few things on which he and "the boss" had disagreed.

Hartmann said he believed the original idea was Jerry Ford's. But of course, he said, "we may have been used, and the White House certainly was not uninterested." He said at that point in history Ehrlichman and Haldeman had been too new to Washington to know all the ins and outs of Congress and definitely had *not* inspired the attack. But he said flatly that "the Justice Department fed us information," that it wasn't "mere raw-file stuff" either, but it never added up to sufficient grounds for impeachment. "Barry Goldwater gave us information, too." Finally, Hartmann said, the Justice Department quit sending information in the fall, "when the White House got an understanding with the Senate that the next appointment to the Supreme Court would be confirmed." Then, Hartmann indicated, the administration lost interest in l'affaire Douglas, and Ford had no recourse but to drop it.

Ford still believed he had made his point, however, that double standards didn't work. The next Nixon appointee, Harry A. Blackmun, was confirmed by the Senate with much less hullabaloo.

The following year Ford was able to take a dispassionate, even a scholarly, view of impeaching judges in a 1971 article he wrote at the request of the *Notre Dame Lawyer*, a law-school review. The article, which Ford himself said he thought was "well done," was entitled "Impeachment—a Mace for the Federal Judiciary." He began with the history of the House of Representatives, in whose early days the mace, or symbol of ultimate authority, was invoked by the Speaker to quell any individual member who became "turbulent." Throughout history no member dared defy such authority once invoked, because the chamber, being sole judge of its membership, could expel any member if it chose to.

Ford likened to the mace the impeachment power of the House and the power of the Senate to try the case. It is interesting that he envisioned it as a mace for the federal judiciary and not for the presidency.

He also noted the heavy influence of British history on the American Constitution, but he cautioned that there are some sharp differences and one of them is in the "divergent view of impeachment." Example: Under the English system the House of Lords can try, convict and sentence any impeached subject, private person or public official, and the lawful penalties ran as high as death. Ford termed American impeachment "relatively mild" because the worst punishment the Senate can impose on a public official is the penalty removing him from office and disqualifying him from ever again holding federal office. Private citizens cannot be impeached.

(Vice President Agnew could have been removed but not sentenced for anything, and he might later have argued double jeopardy if any other prosecution were started—possibly one reason Agnew asked at one point that his case be presented to Congress, some thought.)

The thrust of Ford's article was that impeachment is not the same as criminal indictment. It is a proceeding of an entirely political nature and related solely to the accused's right to hold civil office. It voids any immunity that an accused might claim under the double-jeopardy principle. (Apparently Agnew had not read Ford.)

Ford said the Constitution "clearly established" that impeachment is a unique political device designed explicitly to dislodge from public office those who are patently unfit for it but cannot otherwise be promptly removed. But he said it is one of the most difficult mechanisms in the Constitution and noted it has been used only twelve times in 184 years. In only four of the twelve cases did the Senate convict by the required two-thirds' vote. One official resigned during Senate trial, halting further proceedings.

Next, Ford said, impeachment didn't work out the way the framers of the U.S. Constitution had planned. They were primarily interested in a way to remove a President, protection against arbitrary use of executive power. But as it turned out, he said, all but three of the twelve impeachment proceedings and all four of the convictions involved federal judges. He said the rarity and difficulty of impeachment had led to public misunderstanding. Further, he noted, there was no great body of literature on the subject and that among the members of Congress in 1971, not one Senator and only five imcumbent members of the House were present during the last impeachment trial in 1936 that had resulted in removal of U.S. District Judge Halsted L. Ritter of Florida. (The five House veterans were Leslie Arends, R-Ill.,

Emanuel Celler, D-N.Y., William Colmer, D-Miss., George Mahon, D-Tex., and Wright Patman, D-Tex. Since then both Celler and Colmer have left the House.)

There were, said Ford, four major misconceptions about impeachment:

The first, and in his view most serious of all, was that impeachment is a judicial process. Not at all: It is a political device, not unduly partisan, as it happened, but above all political.

Second, the misconception that federal judges and Justices of the Supreme Court are appointed for life. Ford made the nice distinction that the Constitution provides in its wisdom that they shall hold office "during good behaviour."

Third, that federal judges can be impeached and removed only by being convicted of violating the law, "with all the ordinary protections and presumptions of innocence to which an accused is entitled." He noted one federal judge was successfully impeached for "bringing his court into scandal and disrepute." He said an offense less than a criminal act or criminal dereliction of duty was sufficient. And he declared a higher standard of conduct is actually expected of federal judges than of any other civil officers of the United States. Even so, he claimed the record showed Congress has not misused its power over the judiciary.

Fourth, that impeachment power somehow abrogates the cherished principle of separation of powers —the independence of the judicial, legislative and executive branches from each other. Impeachment is an integral part of the system, he declared, because the "Founding Fathers were practical politicians." The tripartite separation of powers never was "neat or absolute."

"Judicial misbehavior can be reached by the body politic through one method and one method only—impeachment," Ford said.

In the article Ford did not himself define misbehavior. He cited a statement by Senator William G. McAdoo during the trial of Judge Ritter, who was not found guilty of crime but was found unfit for office. McAdoo said, "Not honesty alone, but the punctilio of an honor the most sensitive is then the standard of behavior." One wonders if a majority of the Nixon Supreme Court would have bought that principle as of 1974.

Ford's article was an excellent amassing of historical evidence to support, among other things, his attack on Douglas. In the middle of it he stated tersely, "It is this author's view that conviction of one or more of the offenses cited in Article II is required for removal of the indirectly elected president and vice president, or of appointed civil officers of the executive branch of government"—in other words, the constitutional grounds of "treason, bribery or other high crimes and misdemeanors." Ford avoided discussion of the impeachment and subsequent Senate trial of President Andrew Johnson in 1868, in which the Senate failed by just one vote to remove Johnson from office.

16 Betty

They had always been a happy family, and much of the happiness was associated with their modest but comfortable home at 514 Crown View Drive, Alexandria, Virginia, less than half an hour's drive from the Capitol. Over the years they had formed warm associations with their neighbors. One, although a Democrat, had once bought an ad in the Grand Rapids *Press* at election time to urge fifth-district voters, "Send Jerry back to us; we like him and his family." There was much local pride in Alexandria when Ford was nominated to be Vice President.

December 7, 1973, the neighborhood began to learn some of the practical aspects of a Vice President on the block. The Secret Service moved a big trailer van into the driveway in front of the Ford garage, which was set back from the street less than forty feet. Round-the-clock security for the house commenced, based in the garage, along with the bodyguards who accompanied Ford wherever he went. Bright young Secret Service agents with walkie-talkie radios bustled about the place; special telephone wires lay seemingly at random across the front yard; electronic technicians arrived and departed in trucks full of mysterious equipment. They were as quiet as possible, but in cramped quarters there was no way they could be orderly and neat.

Betty Ford could be quite firm when she felt the need and decreed a quick end to "Operation Improvise" in the driveway and garage. A contractor was called to remodel.

"They [the Secret Service] couldn't care less, but I don't want my neighbors' property values to go down because of us," Betty ruled. The garage was rebuilt into a room for the twenty-four-hour security agents. The front of it was bricked over and given an attractive bay window that provided a clear view up and down the street. The cement driveway was torn up and built anew—reinforced to bear the weight of the Vice President's armored limousine and the Secret Service technical vehicles that came and went on no apparent schedule. The cost of the garage-become-room for the agents' vigil was borne by the government; the cost of the driveway work and a screening wall between it and the house next door was paid by the Fords. They didn't say publicly but it was reported to have cost them more than $5,000. Newsmen, not Jerry or Betty, raised the subject. Betty had foregone a flight to Detroit late in 1973 because it would have taxed the Ford's budget. The occasion was a dinner honoring the great choreographer Martha Graham, who had taught dance to Betty for two years at Bennington College in Vermont and then two more in New York City. Her admiration for Miss Graham was profound and she had been invited to make the presentation of honors. She sent regrets and a telegram of personal appreciation to her old teacher.

The parade of photographers and writers to 514 Crown View continued in early 1974. The Fords kept up their policy of being as available as possible to the daily news media and the special journalists—hoping that in a few months the curiosity that seemed almost worldwide would subside.

The house had been adequate even with four children. It had a small garden and swimming pool in back. When Michael left for the theological seminary in Massachusetts and John had gone to the University of Utah to study forestry, it became almost quiet. Their youngest son, Steven, was active in student affairs at T. C. Williams High School nearby. Susan, sixteen, attended Holton Arms School for Girls in Bethesda, Maryland; she took dancing lessons and worked occasionally in her father's office.

But the vice-presidency changed that quiet atmosphere. While one group of journalists waiting their turn chatted with Secret Service agents outside, another would be inside photographing Betty Ford and asking questions that had become so familiar she could recite the answers almost before the questioner finished a sentence. The new Navy stewards (who came with the vice presidency), Francisco Vasquez and Fernando Yu, came and went on household errands. The telephone jangled and was answered by Nancy Howe, a young woman who had met Susan Ford when they had worked together in the White House Historical Association bookshop. The weekend after Ford's nomination Mrs. Howe had gone to the Ford home to volunteer to help answer telephones; she stayed on as appointments secretary and helpmate to Mrs. Ford and companion to Susan and Steven when the Fords were away at state functions or parties for foreign diplomats—functions that were now de rigueur.

No interview went uninterrupted. Mrs. Ford, looking for her checkbook, said that among other things she was now the family treasurer, and—just a moment while we write one for Fernando to take to the supermarket. ("Be sure to give it to the Safeway manager to be approved first, and don't forget the medicine prescriptions that need to be refilled.")

160

So it went, even on a blissfully sunny day in February when Mrs. Howe's schedule indicated a relatively light day—chiefly a reporter-photographer team from *McCall's* magazine and this writer. Even so, Mrs. Howe made Betty rest a few minutes—after posing more than two hours for a *McCall's* photographer—to eat a sandwich. ("She forgets to eat.")

Those who knew the history were as sparing as possible of Mrs. Ford's energies. Years ago a nerve in her neck had been damaged during some now-forgotten household chore or quick exertion and it had continued to hurt every waking moment. Doctors had never been able to find a cure, they could only prescribe medicines to ease the pain. A psychiatrist was consulted to look for any overlay of psychosomatic aggravation. Ford himself had had three consultations with the psychiatrist during the span of a year to learn whatever a headshrinker could tell an active man, a former athlete, about helping his wife gear down to a new way of life. (Jerry had taught her to ski during their courtship; now both were learning how to begin to grow old.) No one would have blamed the Vice President's lady for leaning a little on the cocktails so often at hand in Washington life, in official and social functions as well as informal. She had tried that, as one experiences many things during a quarter-century in the capital, and was wise enough to know it didn't work. But since Washington was almost as big a gossip mill as Paris, there would always be whispers.

She wore a long, almost formal hostess dress for the benefit of the *McCall's* camera. Her chestnut hair was beautiful. She appeared a little weary but her smile came readily and her eyes flashed at a joke. She had, she revealed, bet Susan five dollars that Jerry would not be the President's choice for Vice President—and

161

paid. Who did she have in mind? Well, perhaps Governor Rockefeller, perhaps Governor Reagan, she said, but without conviction. And definitely not their friend Mel Laird.

"Mel can be abrasive in some situations," she remarked.

She had been asked by many what her system or philosophy had been during the years Jerry had been so busy in Congress or on the road with the military affairs subcommittee, or the Republican campaign and fund-raising circuit. And, as both mother and manager of the house, what was her guideline in raising four children?

"Discipline. Jerry and I both were fortunate to be raised by parents who believed in discipline," she said. "My mother wouldn't let me move to New York to study under Martha Graham until I was twenty years old. After that I went home for six months to think it over before deciding what I was going to do," she said.

"We grew up during the Depression. When I was fourteen, I modeled junior-miss clothing Saturday afternoons in a department store. It wasn't much money, but it was earning something. Everyone took work for granted. There is nothing wrong with work or discipline."

She detailed the achievements of her children. "We are fortunate." She was proud that Steve's most recent report card was all A's except for one B—and he was carrying "six solids" at that. "I went so far as to learn if he had women teachers," she confessed. "He is a charmer." (Mrs. Howe, who had just re-entered the room, bobbed her head in strong agreement.) "But I was told all his teachers are men," Betty added, and laughed at her suspicion. "And Steve does work at his studies."

162

She had enjoyed going home to Grand Rapids with her husband for the "Salute to Jerry" day the previous December. The crush of people at the airport, the camera equipment bumping her head, had been too much for her so she ducked under a rope and "went over to the band, which was playing like mad with nobody paying it any attention. I cheered the band."

She had maintained contact with old friends in Grand Rapids over the years, even with the former wife of one friend whose marriage was tempestuous. "I tried to save that marriage so many times that she begged me to give it up as hopeless," Betty related. "She was great, and he could be charming, but he started playing around with other girls. I saw her last year in Florida, married to a very nice man."

These things happened in Washington, too, Betty learned from long experience. "There are lots of secretaries, lots of temptations." And of course, many long days "downtown," and if needed, many excuses to be away from home.

Wives of Senators were queens in Washington society, Betty noted, while wives of Representatives were, "well, just housewives, and I suppose we were at that." She had good friends in both worlds, however.

She noted wistfully, she and Jerry had come to Washington with the eighty-first Congress in 1949, "and there aren't many of us left." She had talked with her husband about retirement plans and encouraged his decision to run for "just one more term" (she pronounced the phrase with irony in her voice) and then resume his law practice. She said Jerry was so active, had so much energy at sixty, he was really too young to retire. "I want him to retire from one office to another—not even come home for lunch and bother the household. I want him to play

163

lots of golf and enjoy life. But not retire as some people think of it. He's too young for that."

What about 1976? Betty shook her head. "He wanted to be Speaker of the House very much. I'm sorry that could not be. That is what he wanted. We were both so happy for Dick Nixon when he was elected President in 1968—he wanted it so much."

But what if the situation were such, in 1976, that Jerry became convinced it would be best for the nation and the Republican party for him to seek the presidency?

"Then I would accept it. He knows best about those things." Her response was quick; her soft, resonant voice almost took on an edge as she said it. It was an article of faith with her that political decisions were Jerry's.

Then she smiled and added, "But I don't expect it at all. Look at how many there are, all ages, wanting to run for President. You just know it isn't likely to happen that way. Rockefeller and Reagan, both older than Jerry, and Senator Percy, who is younger. There are many."

Had she, even for a moment, thought President Nixon might consider nominating a woman for Vice President?

"No, I didn't. I'm sure Dick felt it's too early for that. I'm for women's lib, but I don't mind walking three paces behind Jerry." She smiled and explained. "That way, if he misses a name at a function or walking along a receiving line, I can pick it up, and we don't have double embarrassment."

The subject evoked a thought, however: "It makes me really angry that women's lib rates him at the bottom of the IQ list. They should look at his staff, with so many women on it. I think they outnumber the men, and they have important jobs." Yes, she agreed, some of them make twenty or thirty thousand dollars a year in salary.

She said she could not remember ever having met Winter-Berger. She dismissed him as an opportunist who had taken advantage of her husband and said, "I think eighty-five percent of the people up there on the Hill, eighty-five percent of the Congressmen, are honest."

Did she feel the White House's presence, now that Jerry was Vice President? Perhaps, sometimes, feel big brother watching?

"Well, I think it would only be good government," was her reply. "There has to be protocol, for instance. I was asked to take the honorary chairmanship of the Blair House committee—the guesthouse for visiting dignitaries, you know. I like it; it seems more roomy and warm than the White House. The White House is so cold. Anyway, I said I would be delighted, but first I would have to check with the White House. Protocol. I learned that Pat Nixon felt she was too busy already and Julie was unable, too. And furthermore, that—at the top—it had already been cleared with the White House for me to accept the chairmanship."

Yes, indeed, she was feeling the vigilant presence of the top power and accepting it as part of her job as well as her husband's.

Then, without being asked a question, of her own volition, she said in a low, musing tone of voice: "Dick surrounded himself with brilliant people, but people who had no experience in government, no congressional background. And they kept other people from seeing him. . . ." Her voice trailed off.

"These tapes," she continued, "I wish [it sounded as if she were going to say "wish to God" but checked herself] they had taken every single one and burned

165

them all right at the start." She had to laugh at the vehemence of her thought.

"I believe Dick," she said simply. "I don't think he knew what they were doing."

She let the interviewer run out of questions and showed no impatience, although she was tired. There was ever so slight a tic that almost rhythmically agitated the extreme left corner of her mouth between her sentences. But she wore her unending pain as a queen would wear a tiara: on straight, under control, with poise and grace.

At the door she willingly entertained a half-jesting thought: If, heaven forbid of course, her husband in turn had to nominate a Vice President, could the biographer come back and discuss with her which women she thought competent for the job?

"I'd be for that!" she said.

17 A Trip Through
Jerry's Mind

"I am the first Eagle Scout Vice President of the United States!"

During an interview with me, Ford said this with pride, as much in having been an Eagle Scout in Grand Rapids high school days as in becoming the first Vice President by nomination to Congress. The Boy Scout Council of America had invited him to speak at a world jamboree of scouts in Hawaii in May. He said he looked forward to attending.

The remark came in a revealing disquisition by Jerry Ford on the career of Jerry Ford. Many politicians are given to explanations for their lives. Lyndon Johnson had been a master of it: "I don't want to be a corn pone—and I don't want to be a big shot in history. All I want is to improve the life of this country and I aim to take a fancy cut at it," Johnson had told reporters one October Saturday in 1964, and he went on to tell how nice it was to look out the bedroom window at the Washington Monument, sleep on silk sheets and draw "four times as much salary as any of you all." Nixon, who had much capacity for self-pity, likened his own role to Great White Father over 210 million people who could behave "like children, if you let them."

Ford, on taking national office, was hailed by the national media as a real Midwest square—anything but astute. He was politician enough to see the advantage in this and realist enough to accept what basis it had. And not to apologize one bit for what he was or had done.

"It didn't bother me at all, really. Because in the first place I didn't think it was true and I don't think there's anything wrong with being typically Midwestern. I heard a commentator say, or I would read what one had written, that I was 'plodding,' or 'dull' or 'noncharismatic.' My answer on a television interview was I'd rather be plodding and get something done than have charisma and accomplish nothing, which is about the best summary I could give."

Was that part of his political philosophy? Definitely yes.

"I've always believed that you take a political job, or get one, you do it; you get another assignment, you do it. And if the ball bounces your way or you get a break, you're prepared for the next assignment, and in the process you've earned the opportunity to qualify. I got on the committee on appropriations, my first real break, because I impressed John Taber, the senior Republican on appropriations. And I got a good subcommittee assignment in two years because Taber thought I did a good job. I then got some favors from Joe Martin [former House Minority Leader] because he had watched, and when the time came to be assigned to the select committee on space, I got it because Joe Martin had observed that I had done a good job. When the time came to be Republican conference [caucus] chairman after the election of 1962, again I had done my homework and I had gained some reputation and the votes were there. Then in 1965, after the '64 election, Minority Leader. So I don't have any hesitancy in standing up for a person who does a job. If he does it well, he

168

merits consideration for the next job. And the mere fact it takes a little time has never bothered me. Too many people in politics get a little impatient."

The act of preparation for the next rung up the ladder was not accidental?

"I never neglected an opportunity to be prepared for the next step. Put it that way."

The traditional scout motto was "Be prepared." Had he enjoyed scouting?

"I'm the first Eagle Scout Vice President of the United States."

Press Secretary Paul Miltich choked a giggle and explained the boss happened to be the first Vice President who had been an Eagle Scout. But the phrase lingered in the mind with the thought that this man had always lived by lessons learned in youth and always would. Washington furnished him a career, but he brought his own values and kept them unchanged.

If the Vice President would tolerate a hypothetical question, what would have to happen before he lost that great loyalty to the President? There was a pause.

"The President has assured me personally—not once but a number of times—that he had no prior knowledge of Watergate, no involvement in the coverup, and I fully believe it. And I am told there is verification in documents and on tapes. I suppose any evidence that undercut that personal assurance would really be about as disappointing as I could imagine. . . . Let me put it this way. I have always tried to deal straight. If somebody asks me a question in politics, I try to give a straight answer. Particularly on matters of such sensitivity and areas of trust. I don't think you can deal at this level unless there is a total faith. And if I was in a position where I misled somebody, I would expect anybody to leave me, extremely disappointed."

There it was, in Ford's phraseology and philosophy. Aide Robert Hartmann had put it more succinctly: If Ford ever became convinced anyone had lied to him, it would be terminal. Ford stressed the word "total." Therefore, there could be no limited trust, or degree of loyalty. Disillusionment would be as total as loyalty had been. A scout was loyal, yes, but to truth, not to falsehood or evil. It was clear Ford considered falsehood and evil synonymous.

Later Ford said in a televised "Face the Nation" program that he had not asked to see the documents or hear the tapes—which the President had assured him were proof of his innocence—for a reason. To have such knowledge might be an advantage to a number-two man; it might conceivably be used to undermine the boss. And, Ford noted, "I am number two."

As long as Nixon remained President newsmen and historians would never cease to question if it were really that simple, to wonder if Ford feared he would find some evil he would rather not know. Not too likely. There was more probably a determination not to have the slightest connection with anything that might later hurt the boss, a real political consideration, and a sensible politician would know it.

There was another consideration in the minds of smart politicians. If you strike a blow at the king, make sure it is mortal. John Dean, new on the rack himself, was learning the awful truth in that old saying. He could only hope the upcoming trials of Mitchell, Ehrlichman and others would vindicate his assertion that the President really had known. If not, Dean could be another Man Without a Country.

Ford himself had nothing whatsoever to lose by his loyalty to Nixon. As long as he believed Nixon, and he gave every sign of believing, he could do what he told innumerable newsmen he wanted: he could be Vice President. Should the king fall by hands of others, President Gerald R. Ford would not have to answer to any man.

Ford insisted he was sincere in saying he had no intention of seeking the presidential nomination of his party. He had always participated in the congressional retirement finance system. After three years at vice-presidential salary his pension would be enhanced. He noted he would be sixty-three at the end of 1976, with "two children through college and the others halfway. We will have the means, and hopefully the health, to do some things I missed out on. I am not doing anything by word or action that is predicated on laying a foundation and building a base for a candidacy in 1976," he said. "I'm doing what is right, not what will do me any good later."

He said he looked forward to the end of the job. "I worked very hard, all the time I've been in politics; I worked hard to get through law school. I think I worked hard in the service. I've really neglected doing a lot of things I really enjoy doing, including spending some time with Betty. Now, we've been lucky—we raised four kids. She has done more than her share in that process. I've been traveling and working long hours. I take stuff home at night, when I'm home. The long and short of it is, I have made a very firm decision I want to catch up on some things that I have missed. And I will be in a position financially because of the retirement program to—in a modest way, with Betty—do some things I want to do.

"I have not gone as far as to say what Sherman did,

171

'neither campaign, nor serve if elected.' I don't think I should, but I am sincere in saying I have no intention of being a candidate in '76. It explains why I can be more frank, why I can be critical one day and supportive the next day, of the President. Because I am not trying to curry favor for a political base in '76."

Ford had other things to say in interviews totaling more than three hours of his carefully managed time. (He had become a very valuable commodity in the administration, not to be wasted with cloakroom chatter.) On the subject of foreign policy Ford said he was now receiving the same daily world-intelligence briefing given the President, twelve pages of it, or more, delivered to him early in the morning. About Southeast Asia: he had known about the invasion of Cambodia before it was launched. "Henry Kissinger called me to the White House and —I was sworn to secrecy—told me what was going to happen." Ford approved of the invasion, of course, felt it might well have been ordered earlier, to deny the army of North Vietnam the Cambodian sanctuaries. The generals had told him how well the enemy was using the Cambodian border and begged for permission to pursue.

In the end he had had to inform Nixon the mood of Congress ("We've got to stop the slaughter") was such that there could be no support for the presence of American troops in Indochina.

"We want no more Vietnams," Ford declared at an interview and even went so far as to say it would be possible, if regrettable, to get along without Cambodia if it should fall to the Communists. But if Saigon and the South Vietnamese government should appear in danger of falling, it would be another matter. Ford said he would not rule out a resumption of the bombing of North Vietnam. "You have to keep your options open."

Ford said one of his most interesting journeys had been the congressional leaders' visit to Red China in 1972. Ford found that Chou En-lai was a charming, polished, shrewd host. "Calculating," Ford added. "Strong. Extremely well-informed." (Mrs. Ford was convinced Chou understood "every word of English" uttered.)

If he had been President, would Ford have sought to reestablish relations with Red China—would he have told a Kissinger to set it up, visit Peking?

"No, not with my record of twenty-three years' opposition. I probably would have been reluctant. But I approve of the policy, and I would hope when the time came, I would have been flexible enough to listen to reasons advanced by a person such as Kissinger. And I must say during these twenty-three years I had a lot of company in both political parties opposing recognition of Red China. Had I been given the arguments I am sure Kissinger gave, I hope my previous unbending policy might have been flexible."

He made it evident he had the highest regard for Kissinger's abilities, and if he were President, he would want the Harvard professor to continue his virtuoso performance as Secretary of State.

He agreed the pace of history—particularly its bad news—seemed to be accelerating. He picked 1965 as the landmark year, without saying it was the year Johnson launched the American ground war in Vietnam. But this did not mean life in the United States had not been good, could not be good in the future, or that progress could not be made in the world. Ford conceded there had been many shocks to the nation's consciousness: inflation, a fuel crisis, "Watergate and all its ramifications."

173

What "ramifications," for instance?

Well, ITT for one. The "milk funds" for another. He felt, "They would not have been investigated, or investigated as thoroughly, had it not been for the Watergate burglary."

Should they have been investigated?

"Yes."

He said the wheat sale to Russia was necessary to help balance trade payments. He conceded, "We might not have been good Yankee traders in the deal." But he did not believe there was any collusion between anyone in the Agriculture Department and the big grain exporters. He said he knew the Ag official who left the department shortly after the deal was made, although he couldn't remember his name. He was sure there was nothing wrong with the deal, other than the American bargainers not being as shrewd as they might have been. On the possibility that Russia might have made an additional coup making buys at less than two dollars a bushel on the commodity-futures market, Ford said, "I'm not that knowledgeable about the market to have an opinion." He repeated that the long history of wheat price supports had resulted in "growing wheat for storage," and the sale at least got rid of what had become a big surplus. "I really feel if there had been anything illegal, the Justice Department would have been forced to take action. My conclusion is we may have been outtraded even though the sale was a good idea."

The way to get enough crude oil, enough energy, in Ford's judgment was to end the oil embargo by the Arabs; then in addition expand American research and development in fields of geothermal and solar energy; and utilize coal in a cleaner way. He said Ralph

174

Nader and other skeptics did a disserve to the public in their claims there was no fuel shortage.

If lightning should strike and he in turn had to name a Vice President, what were his thoughts?

Ford laughed and declared, "The thought never entered my mind."

Ford noted that he was getting a lot of mail, about 500 letters a day. (After the news reports of the Atlantic City speech had had time to sink in, the volume rose to 1,000 a day. Much of it was favorable, some of it urging Ford, "Don't get too close to Nixon." Some expressed a hope Ford might become President. And there were a lot of "vicious, scurrilous" attacks for a variety of reasons.)

If Ford could do just one thing for the American people—one only but the choice his—what would he choose? He thought about it a long time.

"As I look at our problems, anything I could do to restore public credibility and faith in our government. Why do I pick that? Because if the American people have full and strong faith in their government, it gives the leaders of our government bigger clout both at home and abroad. Now I don't mean to say that because our President's popularity is low today, he can't solve the Middle East controversy— because the evidence is his appointee, with his backing, made it possible for a tremendous gain with a negotiated settlement between Egypt and Israel. But generally I think you can say if the American people believe in their leaders, believe in the government, the system, it makes it easier for whoever is running the country to achieve results."

Does it require some positive action by government leaders to bring about this trust and belief?

"To some extent it gets into the question of the

chicken or the egg. I am sure the President's popularity and credibility will go up because Kissinger and he got a negotiated preliminary agreement in the Middle East. [It didn't, at least not in the first post-settlement poll.] So if more things like that will help, the President's position will restore faith in our government. On the other hand, the more backing he gets, the stronger his clout is in dealing with other problems. You always get into that problem of which comes first."

Ford did not demur at the thought that he himself had almost three years to help rebuild that popularity and credibility, nor did he make any comment, because to him it was a part of his job that went without saying. In describing his role as he and the President had discussed it, he said, "The President wants me to be very active with the Congress and expects me to do a great deal of getting out and helping in the political arena. Everything I've been told from the outset has materialized. I see him anytime I want to. I talk to him anytime I want to. And if anything, it's been better than what I envisaged. It's different than what a lot of people thought was the case. People have been disappointed with what Vice Presidents have been told they could do. In my case I'm pleased and optimistic."

But was a "strong" Vice President, a Vice President who marched to his own drum, possible in the American system? No observer of the American system thought so. Ford was regarded by many early in 1974 as an improvement in the President's public relations, an extension of the President's will, and, expressed at its worst, a front man for a basically reclusive President. The public-opinion polls of February, 1974, showed only 26 percent of the electorate felt Nixon was doing a good job; 64 percent believed his performance unsatisfactory; and only 10 percent were in doubt. The last figure was interesting to poll watchers: Seldom was the doubtful group so small.

The bitter and certainly long argument over impeachment had yet to come before the House, although Ford had said he hoped it would be settled (in Nixon's favor, he predicted) by April. The trials of the "big fish," Mitchell and Ehrlichman, for instance, were yet to come. Judge Sirica had not yet finished his grand-jury investigation or stopped his demands for White House evidence.

Many more "bombs" could explode as the Watergate juggernaut ground along Pennsylvania Avenue. It carried the fate of Jerry Ford with it and he was impotent to change its course or halt it.

18 The Future

What kind of President would Jerry Ford be? Fair to adequate, most likely. But it makes no sense to ask the question without also asking, What would be his inheritance? To whom is he compared?

In modern times every new President finds himself guided and shaped not only by his own beliefs and plans, but first by the commitments of his predecessor. Truman presided over the dawn of the atomic era, although he hadn't known what an atom bomb was when he took the oath of office. Eisenhower had to end Truman's war in Korea. Kennedy had to decide on an invasion of Cuba set in train before his presidency; Johnson found himself with commitments to aid Vietnam, give full equality to the nation's blacks and save the big cities; Nixon inherited a war in Vietnam, creeping inflation and a cold war with the Communist world. What kind of legacy was Nixon shaping?

His legacy was ominous. Nixon's verbal State of the Union message to Congress and to the people via television the last of January, 1974, was totally unrealistic. The guts of it were not even in the text. That he was not going to resign, that he would serve out his term, and that "one year of Watergate is enough." His own family in the gallery led a feeble ovation that looked better on TV than it was in actuality. His face perspired freely throughout the forty-seven-minute address, and at one point he faltered badly.

Vice President Ford sat behind and above Nixon at the lectern—unaware that he was just as visible to the millions watching television as the President was. There was a grim, concerned look on his face that did not change throughout the forty-seven minutes. He looked like a Viking chieftain in council at the king's court and much worried about what was to come. Mrs. Ford said she and Susan had chided him for it when he came home. But whatever his thoughts had been, he did not reveal them to his family.

Nixon promised "no recession," although everybody knew one was just around the corner. The President's own economic message two days later pointed to a recession plus inflation. He vowed no gasoline rationing if he could possibly avoid it. Motorists responded by purchasing a few gallons of gas to fill up every time they passed a station that was open.

The truth was many in the nation were behaving as many did on the eve of World War II. There was widespread hoarding of food, of whatever fuel could be hoarded, and of many other items. In suburbia the piles of firewood were twice as big as in the previous winter, and householders admitted it was a feeble hedge against utility failure, a psychological placebo that indicated how thin the public confidence had been drawn. Sophisticates who had the means were buying sailboats, on the theory that gasoline for recreation would be in short supply come summer and powerboating for pleasure might be banned. Resort operators, auto workers, petrochemical workers, plastics makers, to name a few in a wide spectrum of the economy, were experiencing layoffs because of petroleum shortages.

As one auto plant worker, newly laid off, said: "I could care less for about seven months. I will get ninety-five percent of base pay, anyway. Then the unemployment compensation payments and General Motors supplement will stop and things will suddenly get bad, very bad."

Americans were turning in lemming force to the small auto; it would take the Big Three automakers months to convert big-car assembly lines and longer than that to design and build true gas-savers.

There were shortages looming in cotton, copper, zinc, wool, lumber, bauxite, feed grains, beef and even wheat, to name just a few basic commodities in short supply. The nation's wheat reserve was at the lowest in more than a quarter-century. Nixon felt constrained to repeat publicly his vow of "no bread costing a dollar a loaf," although baking-industry leaders had predicted it. The price of gasoline and heating oil kept rising. While the worst was yet to come for millions of Americans, the price inflation was already disastrous for the urban poor, the elderly on Social Security or small pensions, working women who headed families and, of course, the majority of the big-city blacks.

Nixon's Pollyannaesque State of the Union message drew ironic response from working men and women as well as from independent economists and syndicated columnists. If he had any credibility left, that message finished it. A majority of the Congress sat glowering and did not applaud. Perhaps that was why Ford had looked so glum.

The United States *was* in a bad way. Independent truckers were driving unionized contract drivers off the highways with bullets, in protest at diesel fuel prices and falling incomes. Motorists, frustrated over queuing up to buy three dollars' worth, were assaulting gas-station attendants for lack of gas.

There was much opportunistic price gouging here and there in the economy; the Internal Revenue Service seemed unable to halt it.

The American people were coming to be in an ugly mood. They knew how bad things were; they were irritated beyond normal endurance. They were sick of cringing inwardly every time they saw a newspaper headline or heard a news broadcast with more predictions of woe. They were sick of having to wheedle a whole coterie of suddenly important people— gas-pump jockeys, clerks behind a butcher counter, fuel-oil truck dispatchers, insulation contractors, used-car salesmen with Japanese mini-cars on the lot, trash-disposal workers. Suddenly everybody was important except the poor guy who tried to keep his family fed, housed and in school.

And the President came on like Micawber, saying things would get better after about six more months of getting worse.

Never was the ordinary citizen so powerless, nor had he ever been so desperately conscious of that powerlessness at any time since the Depression of the 1930's. Somebody, something, had wrecked "the American way of life"—and it was not him. The Nixon jokes grew in number and viciousness. A mild one was that if the President had been captain of the *Titanic* when it hit the berg, he would have told the passengers they were just stopping to take on ice.

By what logic did the detractors of Jerry Ford's intelligence think he could do worse than Johnson or Nixon? If he just sat in the White House and let Kissinger coddle the Arabs and Israelis, delegated economic policy to competent and honest men, told the truth to the people and raised taxes on economic fat cats, he could become a folk hero.

Timing would be important, of course. If Nixon stepped down voluntarily only a few months after outlining the first $300 billion federal budget, watch out. At the outset Nixon had presented the first $200 billion budget, too. (Five years of Nixon, $100 billion. Whatever became of that 1968 vow of a balanced budget?) If Ford took over early, with almost three years to go and the worst of the economic chickens coming home to roost, then he might by 1976 be another Herbert Hoover—in spite of anything he could do about it. He could not—and by temperament would not—junk Nixon's policies overnight.

Ford was the kind of man who could face up to some tough decisions. Nixon was thinking most of the time about his pride, his own will and his own welfare. Ford was thinking about the nation's wishes and welfare, and the Republican party.

Ford genuinely had no ambition to be President. He would have been a fool not to realize he was closer to it than most Vice Presidents, and improvident if he did not prepare himself for the eventuality. But being prepared was the hallmark of Ford's life. He would not neglect his homework, if the White House gave him any time for it. Ford seemed almost to fear the presidency might come to him without warning, but this is just the feeling of an observer and not provable.

Ford had made it clear that he would retain Secretary of State Kissinger and the foreign policy Kissinger was trying to execute; that he also would continue the detente with Russia and the exploration of normal relations with China. He talked much of "flexibility," as if it were a newly discovered asset. After all, he himself pointed out, for twenty-five years he had represented one congressional district, faithfully, by plan.

When it came to markets and money matters, Ford would have to depend on wise and expert advisers. He had been a small-town lawyer compared to Wall Street or Park Avenue lawyers. He knew next to nothing about commodity-futures markets. He really didn't understand the intricacies of the farm economy or the jungle of the petroleum world.

Ford, the perennial hawk, would continue big military budgets. And he would not hesitate to call a Russian bluff—or fight if he became convinced the time had come to fight or surrender. It had been interesting that Anatoly Dobrynin, Russian ambassador to the United States, visited Ford for a private talk the day after Ford was sworn in as Vice President. Dobrynin had had ten years' experience in Washington and was preparing for any eventuality.

One fears Ford might be even more conservative than Nixon on domestic social programs. He always distrusted the "giveaway" philosophy, as conservative Republicans called it. He would not knowingly let a sparrow starve, but big concepts such as a federally guaranteed personal minimum income just plain scared Jerry Ford. He and Representative Al Cederberg of Bay City had had qualms even about inaugurating federal revenue-sharing with states and municipalities, a program state-level Republicans revered.

If this basic conservatism happened to match the public mood of the time, it would be because the country had turned in its thinking, not because Jerry Ford would change his own philosophy.

He would listen to advisers, to experts in their own fields. Other people were Jerry Ford's books. He was a much more outgoing man than Nixon. And therefore, he would have a better sense of what was going on in the nation, what the people were thinking and saying. He would be capable of walking unexpectedly into the White House press room, putting his hand on a friend's shoulder and asking, "Fellas, was that speech better than Atlantic City?"

But a babe in the woods he would not be. "Poor, dull, Jerry," as Alice Roosevelt Longworth called him, had been in Washington twenty-five years. And he had stayed clean. He, lacking the ambition of a Nixon—and the desire for money that Nixon displayed—could stand up to any monopoly and demand to investigate corporate looting. But he would always believe in a fair return on invested capital, make no mistake there.

Imagination—there was a lack. In Jerry it was, like an appendix, a little-used facility. He much preferred facts. One could understand him believing and saying, as Coolidge had, that the business of America is business.

A friend who knew Ford well for many years said, "How many intellectual Presidents have we had, anyway? Few. And it takes a great moment for a man to be great. No great moment has come to Jerry yet. It is yet obscure to us what his capacity for growth may be. He has a broad knowedge of federal government, broad as that of any man. He has no Bebe Rebozo peering over his shoulder. He has a sense of timing; he's lucky. He's so darned honest. Yet there is an inscrutability about Jerry: You think you know him, but there's always one layer of reserve between you and Jerry's inner self."

Another longtime associate said, "Jerry plays it close to the vest. He doesn't rush to decisions. He talks it over, he thinks it over, he weighs. And then

184

when he has to decide, he decides—and sticks with it. But who knows how he would do as President? Can you say of any man how he would perform?"

But it piques the imagination to wonder how that fierce love of country, that religious dedication to truth, that great loyalty and personal modesty, would translate in the White House. One can almost hear his first major address, for the first time in his life the number-one man rather than a subordinate to someone else. Would he tell his people to put on rose-colored glasses and trust in his regal promise that all would be well? Or would he remain Jerry Ford and call for some effort by all hands to bail out the ship of state and point out just where the leaks were?

But aside from the intangible considerations of patriotism and honor, as President, Jerry Ford would have enormous political clout compared to the agonized Richard Nixon. So many would rush to put their hopes in him.

The monopoly corporations, business, and the right wing of the Republican party would see, if they had any vision or brains left, that here would be American political conservatism's last chance, probably, in this century, that luck had given them what they dreamed of with Goldwater in 1964. If greed could be restrained and the economy fixed up enough to be viable again, here would be a chance to try one more time the old philosophy of pay for what you get.

Ford would have to make some amends to leaders of the AFL-CIO for his Atlantic City speech; it was highly impolitic to lump George Meany in with the ADA when Meany had been a big force in insuring Nixon a landslide in 1972. But wouldn't American labor unions have an interest in a talking relationship with a Ford administration, however short?

185

And if all he did was tell the truth, Ford would have the great majority of the voters hanging on his words. He would have—unless the Nixon legacy became too rancid—a honeymoon, however brief, in which to change some things. And, unlike Nixon, he would have friends in Congress.

Was it not possible in 1974 that the country was ready to trade some glory for stability, some brilliance and rhetoric for confidence? Possible that the nation had enough of adventure and uncertainty, that it wanted off the roller-coaster of prosperity-recession? Possible that it was reaching for a man like Jerry Ford, who had spent a career readying himself to serve somebody else?

9-74

INDEX